Contents

Chapter 1: The housing crisis

Chapter 2: The future of housing

Introduction

HOUSING IN THE UK is Volume 325 in the **ISSUES** series. The aim of the series is to offer current, diverse information about important issues in our world, from a UK perspective.

ABOUT TITLE

For many years, the UK has been in the midst of a housing 'crisis', and this seems unlikely to change in the near future. This book explores the current lack of housing, the challenges to first-time buyers and the changing landscape for tenant and landlords. It also looks at possible solutions for the future, including flatpack housing, using empty buildings and sustainable living.

OUR SOURCES

Titles in the **ISSUES** series are designed to function as educational resource books, providing a balanced overview of a specific subject.

The information in our books is comprised of facts, articles and opinions from many different sources, including:

⇨ Newspaper reports and opinion pieces

⇨ Website factsheets

⇨ Magazine and journal articles

⇨ Statistics and surveys

⇨ Government reports

⇨ Literature from special interest groups.

A NOTE ON CRITICAL EVALUATION

Because the information reprinted here is from a number of different sources, readers should bear in mind the origin of the text and whether the source is likely to have a particular bias when presenting information (or when conducting their research). It is hoped that, as you read about the many aspects of the issues explored in this book, you will critically evaluate the information presented.

It is important that you decide whether you are being presented with facts or opinions. Does the writer give a biased or unbiased report? If an opinion is being expressed, do you agree with the writer? Is there potential bias to the 'facts' or statistics behind an article?

ASSIGNMENTS

In the back of this book, you will find a selection of assignments designed to help you engage with the articles you have been reading and to explore your own opinions. Some tasks will take longer than others and there is a mixture of design, writing and research-based activities that you can complete alone or in a group.

Useful weblinks

www.24housing.co.uk

blog.landregistry.gov.uk

www.bowgroup.org

www.cpre.org.uk

www.theconversation.com

england.shelter.org.uk

www.theguardian.com

GOV.UK

www.hsbc.com

www.huffingtonpost.co.uk

www.ilcuk.org.uk

www.independent.co.uk

propertymoose.co.uk

www.struttandparker.com/housingfutures

visual.ons.gov.uk

www.yougen.co.uk

FURTHER RESEARCH

At the end of each article we have listed its source and a website that you can visit if you would like to conduct your own research. Please remember to critically evaluate any sources that you consult and consider whether the information you are viewing is accurate and unbiased.

Beyond the bricks

The meaning of home.

Some 76% of people who do not own their own home expect to do so in the next five years. *Beyond the Bricks* is HSBC's international study on home ownership, providing insights into how people really feel and behave when buying, renting and owning their own home.

This extract represents the views of more than 9,000 people in nine countries and provides a snapshot of some of the key research findings about millennials' home ownership prospects, the changing role of the home, and the pitfalls of budgeting, around the world.

Millennials and home ownership

Is the dream dead?

Millennials' home ownership ambitions are alive and kicking, but growing affordability challenges look set to defer the dreams of many.

Two in five (40%) millennials around the world own their own home. However, there is significant variation between countries.

Among millennials who don't own, more than four in five (83%) intend to buy a home in the next five years.

But with 64% of millennials who don't own a home needing a higher salary before they can buy, the combination of slow salary growth and rising property prices makes it unlikely that all will be able to achieve their goal.

Seven of the nine countries below are projected to experience real wage growth of less than 2% in 2017.[1]

1 Korn Ferry Hay Group: 2017 Salary Forecast

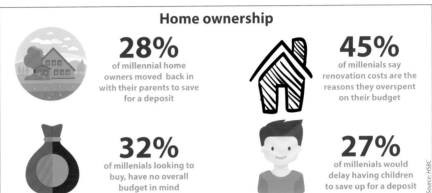

Home ownership

28% of millennial home owners moved back in with their parents to save for a deposit

45% of millenials say renovation costs are the reasons they overspent on their budget

32% of millenials looking to buy, have no overall budget in mind

27% of millenials would delay having children to save up for a deposit

Source: HSBC

Eight of the nine have seen property price rises in 2016.[2]

The affordability challenge is highlighted by the fact that 69% of millennials intending to buy have not yet saved enough for a deposit.

In Malaysia, this figure rises to more than three-quarters (77%) of millennials. This is lowest in the UAE at 45%.

In addition, 34% are being held back because they cannot afford to buy the type of property that they would like

Budget blindness

Millennials also do not have their house in order when it comes to financial planning for their home purchase.

Of millennial non-owners intending to buy a home in the next two years, nearly one in three (31%) have no overall budget in mind and a further 54% have only set an approximate budget.

Those in Mexico are the most likely to have set no overall budget (43%) and those in France the least likely (18%).

Overspending

So it is not surprising that 56% of millennials who bought a home in the last two years ended up overspending their budget.

2 International Monetary Fund: Global House Price Index October 2016 (2016: Q2 or latest, annual per cent change)

This overspend was most common in the UAE and Malaysia (70% and 68%) and least common in France and Canada (41% and 42%).

Overspending

So it is not surprising that 56% of millennials who bought a home in the last two years ended up overspending their budget.

This overspend was most common in the UAE and Malaysia (70% and 68%) and least common in France and Canada (41% and 42%).

Making sacrifices

On the other hand, many millennials are willing to consider making sacrifices to afford their own home.

More than half (55%) of millennials intending to buy would consider spending less on leisure and going out, 33% would be prepared to buy a smaller than ideal place and 21% would consider renting out one of their rooms. E would consider buying with a family member and 11% with friends. More than one in five (21%) would even be prepared to delay having children.

The Bank of Mum and Dad

Financial support from parents can make all the difference when saving for a home. Thirty-six percent of millennial home owners have used the 'Bank of

Mum and Dad' as a source of funding. This was most common in the UAE (50%) and least common in France (26%).

Additionally, one in five (20%) millennial home owners moved back in with their parents to save for a deposit. This was most prevalent in the USA (28%), compared to only six percent in the UAE.

The Bank of Mum and Dad is in demand again when millennials who recently bought a home found they had exceeded their budget.

More than a quarter (26%) borrowed from their family to manage the unexpected costs.

Too little too late

Shaky foundations

Millennials are not the only generation to find the full cost of buying a home higher than they expected.

Thirty-one percent of all non-owners intending to buy in the next two years have set no overall budget. Fifty-three percent have an approximate budget in mind, and only 16% have set a precise one.

Ironically, the least financially prepared to buy in the next two years are those who are currently living rent-free (e.g. with parents), with more than two in five (41%) having no budget in mind.

It should come as no surprise therefore that more than half (53%) of recent home owners found the total cost of buying a home was more than they had budgeted.

Overspending was most common in the UAE and Malaysia (67% and 65%) and least common in Canada and France (32% and 39%).

Unwelcome surprises

Overspending is typically caused by not budgeting for the additional costs of home ownership beyond the property purchase price. Renovation costs (47%) and buying furniture (42%) are the most common reasons why recent home buyers overspent.

This reflects the fact that more than half (56%) of people see their home as their own space, two in five (40%) as a place to make their own and nearly a quarter (23%) as a place to show their own style.

To cope with unexpected costs, 56% of recent home buyers withdrew money from their savings, 42% cut back on their spending, 24% took out a new or larger loan/mortgage, 24% borrowed money from family and 11% borrowed from friends.

Home reinvention

Star quality

Almost two thirds of people (64%) are very happy with their homes, awarding them a 4 or 5 star rating.

Home owners are noticeably happier (74%) than non-owners (55%).

When people were asked what they would do to achieve a 5 star rating for their home, the most popular change was to renovate or modernise (41%).

Seventeen percent would add space or rooms, 14% would choose a quieter or safer area, 10% would like more or improved outdoor space and five percent would add specific features such as a pool.

Location, location, location

When choosing the location of their current home, being in a safe and secure area (39%), good transport links (29%) and the right type of area (26%) were important.

Being close to family was important for more than one in four (22%), while only just over one in ten (12%) mentioned being close to their friends.

Work-life balance

The meaning of home is changing as our homes become places to work as well as places to live.

Half (50%) of millennials work from home and almost a third (29%) would like to, whereas only a third (33%) of baby boomers work from home and only 16% would like to.

Fifty-one percent of baby boomers have never worked from home and do not want to.

Published 2017

⇨ The above information is reprinted with kind permission from HSBC. Please visit www.hsbc.com for further information.

The UK housing market

Summary

⇨ Over the last century, homeownership took off dramatically but the trend is starting to reverse.

⇨ There has been a significant increase in the proportion of renters, particularly at younger ages.

⇨ House prices to earnings are at a record high for first time buyers, partly driven by a lack of supply.

⇨ An increasing number of young adults are living at home with their parents.

⇨ Mortgage lending volumes remain far lower than before the financial crisis.

⇨ There are a number of local authorities on the outskirts of London and the Midlands that have experienced particularly low levels of growth in the supply of housing relative to population change over the last decade.

A century of changing homeownership

⇨ In the early twentieth century, 76% of all households lived in privately rented accommodation.

⇨ But throughout the century there was an increase in homes that were owned, peaking in 2001 at 69%.

⇨ After WWII there was also an increase in the proportion of households living in socially rented accommodation. By 1981, 31% of all households lived in socially rented homes but this declined over the following twenty years.

An Englishman's home became his castle

⇨ Today, housing wealth is the most evenly distributed form of wealth in the UK.

⇨ Housing wealth makes up a large proportion of total wealth for both the wealthiest and least wealthy households.

⇨ For the least wealthy, property accounted for 34% of total wealth in 2012-14, whereas for the wealthiest it accounted for 31%.

⇨ The wealthiest 10% have a higher proportion of their wealth held in financial assets (i.e. savings and bonds) and private pensions than the least wealthy.

⇨ By contrast, the least wealthy have a higher proportion of their wealth held in physical assets (i.e. household possessions including any vehicles).

Retired people are far more likely to be owning a home mortgage free in England

⇨ 72% of retired people own their home outright by comparison to 16% of people working full time.

⇨ 18% of retired households also live in socially rented accommodation.

⇨ Amongst unemployed people, the largest proportion (27%) are living in housing association provided accommodation. There are also just over 13% of unemployed people buying a house with a mortgage.

⇨ This has fallen slightly since the financial crisis in 2008-09 when 16% of unemployed people were paying off a mortgage.

But times...they are a changing

⇨ Since the beginning of the new millennium, the proportion of UK properties that are owner occupied has started to fall – from 69% in 2000 to 63% by 2014.

⇨ At the same time, the proportion of properties privately rented is on the increase – rising from around 9% in 2000 to 19% by 2014.

⇨ Indeed, the number of dwellings in the private rented sector is now bigger than the number provided by housing associations and local authorities combined.

Younger households are increasingly likely to be renters not owners

⇨ The changing nature of homeownership is particularly stark when looking across the generations.

⇨ In the late 1980s, younger people had a good chance of getting on the housing ladder – 65% of people aged 26–30 had a mortgage. By 2014, the proportion of people of the same age with a mortgage had fallen to 42%.

⇨ While the proportion of people with a mortgage falls dramatically with age, there is still a small minority of people with a mortgage between the ages of 65-75 (around 5%).

Rising house prices challenge affordability but prices are not yet back to peak...

⇨ Looking at the difference between nominal and real (inflation adjusted) house prices show stark differences.

⇨ Historical data on real house prices show far greater volatility over time, and suggest house prices are not yet back to peak following the 2008 crisis.

⇨ Both nominal and real data highlight the significant growth in house prices during the late 1990s and early 2000s and the subsequent fall in prices.

⇨ Since 2012 house prices (both nominal and real) have been recovering strongly.

Excluding Germany, house prices have risen faster in the UK after the housing crash than in many other countries

⇨ UK house price appreciation before the financial crisis was particularly strong when compared with a number of other advanced economies.

⇨ While the UK saw a fall in prices after the crash of 2008, prices have recovered faster than in other countries.

House prices are historically high for first-time buyers

⇨ The house price to earnings ratio provides a good indication of affordability. In general, the higher the ratio, the less affordable housing becomes.

- Between 1983 and 2016, first-time buyer house prices have been on average, 3.5 times earnings.

- However, as of Q1 2016, prices were 5.2 times earnings – substantially above the long-run average.

- Today the ratio is close to its pre-crisis peak.

…but beware of dramatic regional differences

- There is a big divide between the south (and in particular London) and the rest.

- While London house prices are far beyond their pre-crisis peak, prices in many regions north of London and the South of England are yet to recover.

- Northern Ireland is a particularly extreme case. By early 2008, property prices in the region were seven times larger than they were just 15 years earlier. But the bubble burst in 2008 and prices fell dramatically and remain way down on their pre-recession peak.

…regional prices impact affordability differently

- London has by far the highest house price to earnings ratio for first-time buyers. Prices are more than ten times average earnings in the capital, making it especially difficult to get on the housing ladder.

- The South West, Outer Metropolitan area and South East (excluding London) also have house price to earnings ratios that are greater than the UK average.

- Scotland has the lowest prices to earnings ratio across UK regions.

While house prices may be higher in London, outstanding mortgages are also much larger

- Outstanding mortgages in London are double the size of those in the Midlands and North of England.

- Outstanding mortgages in London were over £60,000, by comparison to £25,000 in the North East.

- The under-35s bear the largest mortgage debt – averaging £91,000 per person in England.

- By retirement, most have paid off their mortgage debts. Mortgage debt amongst the 65–74 age group averages £4,000 per person.

Very low levels of house building have contributed to the affordability problem…

- After the financial crisis, house building collapsed to less than 150,000 homes being built a year.

- In 2014 (the latest available annual data for the UK), the UK built just 145,000 new homes. This contrasts with over 400,000 new homes at the peak in the late 1960s.

- Local authority house building led to the substantial increase in supply in the post-war era.

- The private sector has only occasionally built more than 200,000 homes over a 12-month period.

…as well as to comparatively lows levels of mortgage lending

- The number of mortgage approvals remains way down relative to the pre-crisis period.

- At the peak, in the latter half of 2003, there were over 300,000 mortgage approvals, boosted by a substantial amount of remortgaging and other activity alongside a relatively high number of approvals for purchase.

- By contrast, since the recession we have been averaging just over 100,000 approvals per month with substantially less remortgaging and other mortgage lending activity.

…reduced affordability has led to increasing numbers of young adults living with their parents

- The number of young adults living at home with their parents has markedly risen over the last two decades.

- Between 1999 and 2014 the number living with their parents rose by one million – faster than the rate of population growth for that age group.

- As a result a record 6.7 million young adults lived with their parents in 2014 – this fell slightly to 6.6 million in 2015.

July 2016

- The above information is reprinted with kind permission from the ILC-UK. Please visit www.ilcuk.org.uk for further information.

Five facts about… housing

The steady rise in the cost of buying a home shows no sign of abating, as ONS figures reveal that average house prices have risen by 8.7% in the year to June 2016.

But house prices are just one part of the story; here are five facts about housing in the UK, from renting to the number of homes being built.

1. The average UK house price was £214,000 in June 2016

This average price is £24,000 above its pre-economic downturn peak of £190,000 in September 2007.

2. The percentage of 25- to 29-year-olds owning their home decreased from 55% in 1996 to 29% in 2015

The percentage of 30- to 34-year-olds owning their home decreased from 68% to 45%, between 1996 and 2015.

3. All the countries that constitute Great Britain have experienced rises in their private rental prices since 2011

Since January 2011 England rental prices have increased more than those of Wales and Scotland.

4. In 1995, the cheapest small area in England and Wales to buy a property was in the Alexandra Park area of Manchester

The average (median) price of £9,000. In 2015, the cheapest area was in the Pendle district of Lancashire, at £30,000.

5. The overall level of house building in the UK has declined since 1980, with 152,380 houses built in the financial year ending 2015

This represents a fall of nearly 40% from the 251,820 built in the financial year ending 1980. New data for 2015/2016 from England and Northern Ireland suggests that the recent increase in UK house building is continuing.

17 August 2016

⇨ The above information is reprinted with kind permission from the Office for National Statistics. Please visit visual.ons.gov.uk for further information.

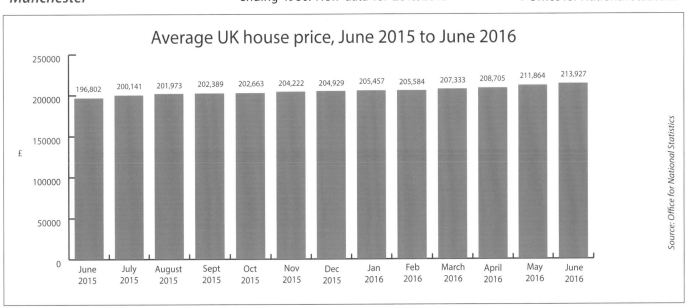

Average UK house price, June 2015 to June 2016

Month	Price (£)
June 2015	196,802
July 2015	200,141
August 2015	201,973
Sept 2015	202,389
Oct 2015	202,663
Nov 2015	204,222
Dec 2015	204,929
Jan 2016	205,457
Feb 2016	205,584
March 2016	207,333
April 2016	208,705
May 2016	211,864
June 2016	213,927

Source: Office for National Statistics

The shortage of affordable homes

The country is in the grip of a housing shortage. And soaring rents, poor conditions and rising homelessness are the end result.

Shelter provides support and advice 365 days of the year to those facing bad housing or homelessness. But we know we will never fix the root causes of the problem unless we build enough decent, affordable homes.

For decades, successive governments have failed to build the homes we need. By 2008, the number of new homes being started had fallen to its lowest peacetime level since 1924 – and house building has barely recovered since then.

This means that every year more and more people are being priced out of home ownership. It means rising rents and more people competing for every single home.

What is a decent home?

A home is more than just a roof over your head. It's the place where you can bring up a family, put down roots and thrive. Shelter believes there should be a decent, affordable home for everyone.

But every day we hear about families and households who are denied this, often through no fault of their own. Dreadful conditions that endanger a child's health; the constant worry of eviction that prevents a couple from starting a family; or ever-rising bills that put a family at risk of homelessness.

We work to make sure these fears are removed and these problems are fixed. We campaign to make sure that everyone can find and keep a home in a decent condition.

A home should be in a decent condition

Shelter believes every home should be safe to live in. That means it must be clean, dry and free of hazards, such as dangerous electrics. Yet nearly three in ten (29 per cent) private rented homes in England fail to meet the Decent Homes Standard[1].

With a lack of decent housing available, and not enough safe new homes being built, thousands of families have no choice but to live in appalling conditions that put their health in danger.

We want more done to improve the quality of housing, and we want better standards to be enforced nationally.

A home should provide stability

Shelter believes that for a house to be a home, it must be stable. It has to give families and households a chance to settle down, safe in the knowledge that they won't be evicted or forced to move on before they're ready to leave.

Many homeless people face a life of constant upheaval and a lack of stability as a result of the homes they end up in. More than 120,000 children were homeless and living in temporary accommodation in Britain in December 2016[2]. That means families being moved from place to place, living in hostels and B&Bs, constantly waiting to hear if they'll have a place to move on to.

The surge in private renting has also seen security and stability eroded for millions of renting families. Eleven million people in England now rent their home from a private landlord, including 1.6 million families. With short-term contracts the norm, many private renters live continually with the fear of eviction, afraid they may wake up to find their landlord has forced them to leave their home and local community. Private renting families are almost eight times more likely to move than homeowners, and almost half worry about their landlords ending their contract before they are ready to go.

A home should be affordable

The lack of affordable housing is getting worse, with prices growing further out of reach. In one in four areas private rents went up by more than £300 in 2012. And things are just as bad

for those looking to buy; average house prices in England are now eight times average earnings[3].

With bills continuing to soar and incomes stagnating, rising housing costs can be the final straw that pushes a household into arrears, or even homelessness. In 2016 over 50,000 private renting households in England and Wales were put at risk of losing their home[4].

For many, the problem is not just the amount that must be paid in bills, but the unpredictability that comes with renting. With most contracts in the private rented sector, after six months a landlord can raise the rent to any amount they like without very little warning. Similarly, letting agents can charge fees at any point in the tenancy. Those who are struggling to get by may be forced over the edge by an unexpected bill or a huge rent rise, and could face debt, eviction or even homelessness as a result.

Shelter's view

We want to see housing costs made more affordable. This would be helped by more predictable rent increases for those who privately rent, as well as proper support and advice for those with a mortgage.

And we want to see standards improved in the private rented sector, to provide renters with better homes that don't put them at risk.

⇨ The above information is reprinted with kind permission from Shelter. Please visit england.shelter.org.uk for further information.

© Shelter 2017

1. English Housing Survey, Headline Report, 2015/16 https://www.gov.uk/government/statistics/english-housing-survey-2015-to-2016-headline-report

2. Department for Communities and Local Government, Live Tables on Homelessness, Table 770; Stats Wales, 'Homelessness statistics', Scottish government 'Homelessness statistics' https://www.gov.uk/government/statistical-data-sets/live-tables-on-homelessness

3. Median house price data for 2016 from ONS/Land Registry and median total gross annual salary data for 2016 from the Annual Survey of Hours and Earnings (ASHE)

4. These are households in England issued a possession notice by a mortgage lender or landlord. The first step to losing their home. Ministry of Justice Mortgage and Landlord Possession Statistics: https://www.gov.uk/government/collections/mortgage-and-landlord-possession-statistics

Social problems caused by house price inflation

By Daniel Rossall Valentine

Sustained house price inflation creates a number of major social problems including the following:

1. **Growth of the proportion of rental properties and decline in the proportion of properties that are available for purchase.** This is an almost automatic phenomenon caused by house prices going beyond the level that people can borrow, and deposits also escalating. In these conditions, investment buyers become much more powerful in the market, and can use this power to amass large portfolios of homes, which are then offered for rent.

2. **Overcrowding.** Overcrowding is one of the many tangible impacts of the housing crisis on households across the country. Data from the Office for National Statistics shows that homes with six residents are the fastest growing category of household and three million people in the UK now live in a home with at least five other individuals. In a period of price inflation, tenants are increasingly forced to sublet communal rooms as bedrooms in order to cover rent inflation.

3. **Delayed home-owning.** Young people trapped in rented properties or parental homes till mid-life; facing delay in starting families and restrictions on the other freedoms associated with security of tenure, such as the ability to entertain guests and the freedom to refurbish living quarters to personal taste. According to PwC, the proportion of young people (aged 20–39) who own a home (or have a mortgaged property) will fall from 38% (2013) to 26% by 2025. As a consequence, the number of young people who rent a property is set to rise from 45% (2013) to 59%. The number of people who want to own a house but are unable to get onto the housing ladder (the home-ownership gap) has been estimated at five million people. According to the ONS, across England, two million adults are still living with their parents. Calling this "delayed" home-owning is rather euphemistic, since unless the problem resolves, most of these people will never be able to own a house. House prices continue to rise faster than wages and so the bar for the deposit will keep moving upwards.

4. **Smaller properties.** The house price crisis encourages builders to construct smaller and smaller properties, in order to create 'affordable homes', and to maximise the profit from the diminishing amount of available land. According to RIBA, the average one-bedroom new-build home is currently 46 sq metre, the size of a carriage on London Underground's Jubilee Line. The average floor space for a property in the UK as a whole is currently 85 sq metres – making UK homes the smallest in the EU, and less than half the size of average houses in Australia, Canada or the US.

5. **Residential segregation.** Further segregation of urban areas, with domestic owner-occupiers squeezed out from the well-heeled areas that are most attractive to investors.

6. **'Landlordism'.** Landlordism represents a collection of problems associated with the rental of properties to low-income households, and the unpleasant tactics that landlords use when faced with tenants who have few choices. Landlordism is associated with overcrowding, insecurity of tenure and poor maintenance of property.

7. **Emigration.** Emigration has never been higher than it is now, with many young people realising that the only way of owning a house is to leave the UK. The emigrants tend to be educated above average, and this represents a brain drain.

8. **Escalation of government spend on housing benefit.** One of the stated goals of the 1980 'right to buy' policy was to reduce spend on housing. It was initially successful in this goal, but the rapid rise in housing benefit spend between 1990 and 2012 has negated this cost-saving.

9. **The further elimination of parks and playing fields, as recreational spaces yield to the remorseless activity of property developers urged on by escalating land values.** Rising house prices places socially useful land under threat including the preservation of historic buildings.

10. **A reduction in duration of tenure.** Rising prices tend to increase the turnover rate of flats, since landlords will try to increase rents and many tenants will not be able to afford these rent rises and will therefore be forced to 'downshift' i.e. locate a cheaper flat. Frequent relocation is disruptive for anyone, but is particularly disorientating for children.

November 2015

⇨ The above information is reprinted with kind permission from The Bow Group. Please visit www.bowgroup.org for further information.

Home ownership in England at a 30-year low, official figures show

English Housing Survey finds private rented sector doubled in size since 2004, with ownership at lowest level since 1985.

Home ownership in England has fallen to its lowest level for 30 years, while the number of people privately renting is now higher than in the early 1960s, according to official figures.

Government data reveals that the private rented sector has doubled in size since 2004, with almost half of all people in England aged 25 to 34 paying a private landlord for their accommodation.

Ministers recently admitted England's housing market was "broken", with home ownership a distant dream for millions.

Labour claimed the figures showed that the Government was "out of ideas" and had no long-term plan to fix the housing crisis. The Generation Rent campaign group said runaway house price inflation and the difficulty of saving a deposit had trapped millions in private rented housing, "even more [people] than in the days of slum landlords like Rachman".

The latest English Housing Survey, produced by the Department for Communities and Local Government (DCLG), found that of the estimated 22.8 million households in England, 14.3 million– or 62.9% – were owner-occupiers in 2015–16.

It stated that owner-occupation rates "remain unchanged for the third year in a row" – but Labour and others were quick to seize on an accompanying table, which showed that the rate had slipped from 63.6% the previous year. This is down from a peak of 70.9% in 2003 and is the lowest figure since 1985, when it was 62.4%.

By contrast, the private rented sector has ballooned in size and now accounted for just over 4.5 million households – double the 2.3 million in 2004. The new figure represents 20% of the total, whereas in 2002 it was 10%.

Separate government data shows there were 4.377 million private rented households in England in 1961.

The English Housing Survey said that, while younger people had always been over-represented in the private rented sector, over the past decade the increase "has been particularly pronounced". In 2005–06, 24% of those aged 25–34 were privately renting. This figure has now leapt to 46%.

Over the same period, the percentage of those in this age group buying a home with a mortgage plummeted, from 53% to 35%.

The report also revealed a surge in the number of children growing up in a privately rented home rather than one owned by their parents. It estimated that there were now about 945,000 more households with dependent children in the private rented sector than there were a decade ago. Meanwhile, the number of households with children in the social rented sector was about 123,000 less than ten years ago.

In 2015–16 the average private rent in London was £300 per week, about double the £153 figure for outside the capital. On average, those buying their home in England with a mortgage spent 18% of their household income on mortgage payments, whereas rent payments were 28% of household income for social renters, and swallowed up 35% of household income for those renting privately.

It also emerged that levels of overcrowding as measured by the so-called "bedroom standard" have increased in the social rented sector. At the same time, the proportion of homes judged to be "under-occupied" that were owned by the person living there had risen from 39% (5.3 million households) in 1995–96 to 52% (7.4 million households) now.

The report also provided fresh

evidence that, for those who can afford to buy, the traditional 25-year mortgage may be on the way out. It found that almost all first-time buyers had taken out a repayment mortgage, and that 40% had signed up for a home loan lasting 30 years or more. The average age of a first-time buyer now is 32, up from 31 in 2005–06.

Responding to the figures, John Healey, the shadow housing secretary, said: "After seven years of failure on housing, not only has home ownership fallen, but affordable housebuilding has hit a 24-year low, and rough sleeping has more than doubled."

Dan Wilson Craw, director of Generation Rent, said: "The Government knows that the housing market is broken but it is failing to do enough to fix it. Ministers need to expand their ambitions to build homes, while reforming the law to provide stability for the millions who will be unable to buy in the foreseeable future."

However, in its white paper the Government promised a fresh wave of homebuilding. It said the number of home completions in England had been lower than anywhere else in Europe, relative to the population, for the past three decades.

The DCLG indicated that a fall in the proportion of owner-occupiers from 63.6% in 2014–15 to 62.9% in 2015–16 was not statistically significant, hence its statement in the survey that "owner occupation rates remain unchanged for the third year in a row".

2 March 2017

⇨ The above information is reprinted with kind permission from *The Guardian*. Please visit www.theguardian.com for further information.

Britain's housing market is in poor health, but it's not just a shortage – here's why

An article from The Conversation.

By Kenneth Gibb, Professor of Housing Economics, University of Glasgow

THE CONVERSATION

The UK's housing market is in critical condition. The symptoms are stark: demand in several regions far outstrips supply, prices relative to earnings in many major cities are beyond the reach of most people, home ownership is increasingly unobtainable, the homeless population is growing and low-income households are too often having to settle for substandard homes.

Yet so far, an exact diagnosis has proved elusive and, as a result, effective treatment has not been administered. The problem is that the housing sector is often described in shorthand – the housing market, "affordable" housing, the neighbourhood or council housing, to name just four such ways of talking about housing. Each is quite different and even just looking at any one masks more than it illuminates – there is considerable variation in the quality and attractiveness of council housing, for instance.

Housing is a complex, interdependent system, with many components of different types and scales. Its function isn't isolated from its environment – the operation of the housing system is closely connected to the land market and planning mechanisms as well as the construction and development industries. And housing exists across a range of jurisdictions and tenures, each accompanied by different laws, rights and obligations.

Living history

The housing system has also been moulded by history. For one thing, much of the UK's housing stock is with us as part of a long-established and enduring built environment. It has also been shaped by extensive and overlapping sets of more or less effective government interventions over time: from the garden city movement, to post-war slum clearance, Margaret Thatcher's Right to Buy and many others. These policies are situated amid shifts and changes in cultural beliefs about housing, aspirations and material constraints.

Housing systems are affected by economic change and income growth at local and regional levels – as well as interest rates, regulation of mortgage lending, housing taxes and other policies that privilege one set of housing arrangements over another. Demography – encompassing trends in migration, household size and ageing – also contributes to the shape and size of housing demand.

Yet these relationships run both ways. Housing is such a critical consideration for political and economic decisions that the state of the sector directly affects the economy and demography of the UK, as well as being affected by them. In a housing bust, for instance, falling incomes can reduce demand and house prices. But if house prices continue to fall, this can also reduce consumption and spending, as people feel worse off.

Unpicking the threads

When you think about housing as a system, it becomes clear that the 'housing crisis' is actually a collection of symptoms from several chronic, overlapping problems. The UK housing market has experienced decades of privileged taxation treatment. Consecutive governments have been obsessed with boosting rates of home ownership. Meanwhile, the development industry's business model is based on lifting land value, with planning permission from local authorities, which results in the construction of more expensive properties. And there has been long-term under-investment in social and affordable housing, combined with an over-reliance on welfare benefits to offset rising rents.

We know that the housing system is dominated by the existing stock, so it stands to reason that it will take a long time to untangle and address these issues, which have built up over the decades. That is, assuming that political consensus is strong enough to allow coherent long-term policy to move forward in step. This is a fair definition of a 'wicked' problem.

To build consensus and tackle these issues, housing policy and practice need to be based on evidence, which is grounded in this systemic point of view. The evidence will need to be nuanced, according to the great variety in the sector across the UK: after all, housing is largely devolved, and significant differences between the situations and approaches in Scotland, Northern Ireland, England and Wales are already apparent. For instance, there is no Right to Buy in Scotland – instead, a new private tenancy law will produce longer-term tenancies that may yet encourage more families into the rented sector.

To this end, the University of Glasgow, together with eight other UK universities and four non-academic partners, is embarking on an ambitious programme: the UK Collaborative Centre for Housing Evidence (CaCHE). Our aim is to put evidence and analysis back at the heart of this complex social and economic problem. This research will provide the ammunition to influence and transform housing policy and practice through better problem diagnosis, policy evaluation and appraisal of new opportunities, in order to generate improved housing outcomes for all.

7 April 2017

⇨ The above information is reprinted with kind permission from *The Conversation*. Please visit www.theconversation.com for further information.

Private renting

Your rights and responsibilities

You have certain rights and responsibilities if you're a tenant in privately rented property.

Your rights

As a tenant, you have the right to:

⇨ live in a property that's safe and in a good state of repair

⇨ have your deposit returned when the tenancy ends – and in some circumstances have it protected

⇨ challenge excessively high charges

⇨ know who your landlord is

⇨ live in the property undisturbed

⇨ see an Energy Performance Certificate for the property

⇨ be protected from unfair eviction and unfair rent

⇨ have a written agreement if you have a fixed-term tenancy of more than three years.

If you have a tenancy agreement, it should be fair and comply with the law.

If you don't know who your landlord is, write to the person or company you pay rent to. Your landlord can be fined if they don't give you this information within 21 days.

When you start a new tenancy

When you start a new assured or short assured tenancy, your landlord must give you:

⇨ a copy of the *How to rent* guide if you live in England

⇨ a tenant information pack if you live in Scotland

Your responsibilities

You must give your landlord access to the property to inspect it or carry out repairs. Your landlord has to give you at least 24 hours' notice and visit at a reasonable time of day, unless it's an emergency and they need immediate access.

You must also:

⇨ take good care of the property, for example turn off the water at the mains if you're away in cold weather

⇨ pay the agreed rent, even if repairs are needed or you're in dispute with your landlord

⇨ pay other charges as agreed with the landlord, for example Council Tax or utility bills

⇨ repair or pay for any damage caused by you, your family or friends

⇨ only sublet a property if the tenancy agreement or your landlord allows it.

Your landlord has the right to take legal action to evict you if you don't meet your responsibilities.

If your landlord lives outside the UK

Contact HM Revenue and Customs (HMRC) if your landlord lives outside the UK and you pay £100 or more a week in rent directly to them.

You may have to deduct tax from your rent under HMRC's 'non-resident landlord scheme'.

Document checks

You must prove that you have a right to rent property in England if you're:

⇨ starting a tenancy on or after 1 February 2016

⇨ renting it as your main home.

Exemptions

You won't have to prove your right to rent if you live in:

⇨ student accommodation, for example halls of residence

⇨ accommodation provided by your employer as part of your job or training

⇨ social housing

⇨ accommodation provided by the council

⇨ hostels and refuges

⇨ a care home, hospital or hospice

⇨ accommodation with a lease of seven or more years

What your landlord must do

Your landlord (or letting agent) must:

⇨ check your original documents to make sure you have the right to rent a property in England

⇨ check the documents of any other adults living in the property

⇨ make copies of your documents and keep them until you leave the property

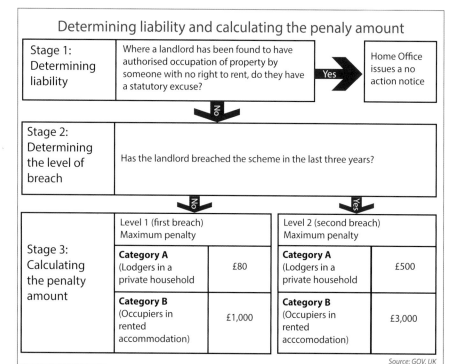

Determining liability and calculating the penaly amount

Stage 1: Determining liability	Where a landlord has been found to have authorised occupation of property by someone with no right to rent, do they have a statutory excuse?	**Yes** →	Home Office issues a no action notice

No ↓

Stage 2: Determining the level of breach	Has the landlord breached the scheme in the last three years?

No ↓   Yes ↓

Stage 3: Calculating the penalty amount	Level 1 (first breach) Maximum penalty		Level 2 (second breach) Maximum penalty	
	Category A (Lodgers in a private household	£80	**Category A** (Lodgers in a private household	£500
	Category B (Occupiers in rented accommodation)	£1,000	**Category B** (Occupiers in rented acccomodation)	£3,000

Source: GOV.UK

⇨ return your original documents to you once they've finished the check

Your landlord must not discriminate against you, for example because of your nationality.

If you can't prove your right to rent

You won't be able to rent property if you can't provide the acceptable documents.

If the Home Office has your documents

If the Home Office has your documents because of an outstanding case or appeal, ask your landlord to check with the Home Office.

Give your landlord your Home Office reference number to do the check.

If your circumstances mean you can still rent in the UK

In some circumstances, you can still rent even if you aren't allowed to stay in the UK, for example if you're:

⇨ a victim of slavery

⇨ using the Home Office's voluntary departure scheme.

Check with the Home Office team that's dealing with your case.

Your landlord will have to check with the Home Office.

Repeat checks

You won't have a further check if you stay in the same property and either:

⇨ you're British or from an EEA country

⇨ you have no time limit on your right to stay in the UK.

Your landlord will have to make a repeat check if there's a time limit on your right to stay in the UK.

Your landlord will ask to see your documents again just before your permission to stay runs out, or after 12 months, whichever is longer.

Your landlord's safety responsibilities

Your landlord must keep the property you live in safe and free from health hazards.

Gas safety

Your landlord must:

⇨ make sure gas equipment they supply is safely installed and maintained by a Gas Safe registered engineer

⇨ have a registered engineer do an annual gas safety check on each appliance and flue

⇨ give you a copy of the gas safety check record before you move in, or within 28 days of the check.

Electrical safety

Your landlord must make sure:

⇨ the electrical system is safe, for example sockets and light fittings

⇨ all appliances they supply are safe, for example cookers and kettles.

Fire safety

Your landlord must:

⇨ follow safety regulations

⇨ provide a smoke alarm on each storey and a carbon monoxide alarm in any room with a solid fuel burning appliance (for example a coal fire or wood-burning stove)

⇨ check you have access to escape routes at all times

⇨ make sure the furniture and furnishings they supply are fire safe

⇨ provide fire alarms and extinguishers if the property is a large house in multiple occupation (HMO).

Deposits

You may have to pay a deposit before you move in. Contact your local council about possible rent or deposit guarantee schemes if you're having difficulty paying the deposit.

Deposit protection

Deposit disputes

Contact the deposit protection scheme your landlord used if you can't get your deposit back.

⇨ The above information is reprinted with kind permission from GOV. UK.

© Crown copyright 2017

Private tenants are putting up with dangerously cold homes, scared of eviction if they complain

*An article from **The Conversation.***

THE CONVERSATION

By Aimee Ambrose, Senior Research Fellow, expert in domestic energy efficiency, Sheffield Hallam University

Struggling tenants living in private rented accommodation are enduring dangerously cold homes and high heating bills. Our new research has found this is largely because they fear that asking their landlord to make improvements – such as installing more efficient heating or double glazing – might lead to rent increases or eviction.

The private rental sector in England is the fastest growing type of accommodation in the country, as home ownership becomes increasingly out of reach for young people and social housing more scarce. The sector also houses a higher proportion of poor and vulnerable households than any other tenure and these groups are among the least likely to speak out against poor conditions.

But living in cold accommodation that is difficult to heat can be a threat to health. Evidence to a 2012 parliamentary enquiry from the National Private Tenants Organisation suggested that 15% of private rented properties were so cold that they posed an immediate threat to health.

Rationing the heating

My research, with 50 people in England, found that rather than lobby landlords for improvements, tenants try and cope with cold homes by rationing heating, sometimes to as little as ten or 20 minutes a day, wearing outdoor clothing inside, spending extra time in bed or more time outside the home. The majority of the people I spoke to were employing a combination of these coping mechanisms. One person I interviewed in Hackney, north London, said:

"It's [expletive] cold, I put the duvet round me and just lie in bed, it's not productive."

While tenants continue to tolerate cold homes, landlords will feel little pressure to address poor energy performance. But tenants are scared to speak out.

Among those I spoke to, private renting was no one's first choice. An overheated rental market is leading tenants to compromise over the quality of the homes they choose, with many forced to accept the first place that they could afford. One tenant in Rotherham, South Yorkshire, told me:

"It was the first one I looked at and it was horrible, it was freezing… but they were the only landlords that I dared go to cos I think I would have failed a credit check."

In the scramble to find somewhere to live, tenants overlook the signs that a property would be cold and difficult to heat. This leaves them with little bargaining power as in a buoyant rental market, low-income tenants are in a weak position to make demands of landlords. Tenants in London are particularly aware that their landlord could replace them tomorrow with someone willing to pay more rent than they could. So they often try to avoid troubling the landlord for anything, in the hope of avoiding rent increases or eviction.

Scared of what might happen

We found the relationship between tenants and landlords was characterised by fear. Pre-payment meters which require advance payment for heat and energy, are a case in point. Over half of those I surveyed lived in properties with these meters, but because paying for energy via this method costs more than paying monthly or quarterly, some tenants wanted them removed. But this requires the landlord's permission and most people who wanted their meter removed were too afraid to ask out of fear that their rent would go up.

Despite widespread dissatisfaction with living in cold homes, 47 of the 50 people I surveyed had not sought any help or advice. This was due to both a fear of having to involve the landlord and not knowing where to turn. They were rarely aware of schemes which provide subsidised energy efficiency measures to landlords, such as the Energy Company Obligation.

We found that there were emotional consequences of living in a home that makes you unhappy and where you feel insecure. Participants were stressed about meeting high heating costs, and were eating poor quality food to free up money for heating. Yet dealing with the consequences of this was considered preferable to the prospect of eviction.

Improving the experience of low-income private renters will require a greater understanding of what drives landlords' investment decisions. A combination of tougher regulation of the sector is needed, coupled with carefully targeted incentives to compel landlords to invest in making their properties more energy efficient.

7 February 2017

⇨ The above information is reprinted with kind permission from *The Conversation*. Please visit www.theconversation.com for further information.

Typical tenant pays £40,000 in rent over five years, report finds

Research by Shelter highlights high cost of renting as Lords debates bill that charity claims will exacerbate housing shortage.

By Heather Stewart

The typical tenant in England has spent more than £40,000 on rent over the past five years, according to new research published on Thursday by homelessness charity Shelter, in time for the housing bill debate on the same day in the House of Lords.

Shelter says that the average cost of renting a two-bedroom home is enough to put down a 20% deposit on the average first-time buyer home. In London, the average rent for a two-bedroom property has been far higher, at £89,000, the charity calculated.

Campbell Robb, Shelter's chief executive, said: "Our drastic shortage of affordable homes is leaving millions of people stuck in their childhood bedrooms in a bid to save money, or in expensive and unstable private renting with little hope of ever saving for a home to put down roots in."

The housing and planning bill making its way through the Lords introduces a series of changes which David Cameron has said will "turn generation rent into generation buy", including the right for social housing tenants to buy their properties. Shelter says it will exacerbate the housing shortage.

Local authorities must fund the policy by selling off high-value council properties in their local area, but peers are warning that the policy could lead to a collapse in the supply of affordable homes. Cross-bench peer Lord Kerslake, former head of the Government's Homes and Communities Agency, said: "It's very hard to make the numbers work; and it's very hard to find the land."

Kerslake has jointly tabled an amendment to the housing and planning bill which would force councils to replace the properties sold off in this way with similar homes in their own area.

Peers are also concerned about the Government's starter home initiative. These new-build properties will be sold at a 20% discount to homebuyers under the age of 40, at anything up to £450,000 in the capital, or £250,000 outside.

By urging developers to prioritise starter homes, there are fears local authorities will crowd out genuinely affordable housing. Kerslake said the policy would be a "cash bonanza" for homebuyers, many of whom could have purchased their own home without the scheme.

"It's a hell of an offer for people who have to be reasonably well-heeled to afford it," he said.

Research by the Town and Country Planning Association has found that four out of five councils do not believe starter homes should be classed as affordable.

Dame Kate Barker, who carried out a review of housing supply for Gordon Brown, told the Lords economic affairs committee in December, "I do feel uncomfortable about a set of policies that are designed to be supportive of people who are just on the cusp of being able to buy, and need nudging over the edge."

The shadow housing minister, John Healey, said: "The forced sale of council homes will lead to a huge, irreversible loss of genuinely affordable homes to buy and rent. At a time when more affordable homes are desperately needed, the Government is forcing the sale of many of those that are left – not to tenants but to buy-to-let landlords and overseas speculators.

"This will make finding an affordable home even harder for young people and families on ordinary incomes. But it's also bad news for taxpayers because it means more people renting privately and housing benefit rising to cover the cost."

A spokesman for the Department for Communities and Local Government said: "The Government is also supporting the boldest plan for housing by any government since the 1970s and is creating a bigger, better private rented sector that will increase choice for tenants."

3 March 2016

⇨ The above information is reprinted with kind permission from *The Guardian*. Please visit www.theguardian.com for further information.

Housing crisis threatens a million families with eviction by 2020

Report shows combination of low wages, freezes to benefits and rising costs of renting could cause more than one million households to become homeless.

More than a million households living in private rented accommodation are at risk of becoming homeless by 2020 because of rising rents, benefit freezes and a lack of social housing, according to a devastating new report into the UK's escalating housing crisis.

The study by the homelessness charity Shelter shows that rising numbers of families on low incomes are not only unable to afford to buy their own home but are also struggling to pay even the lowest available rents in the private sector, leading to ever higher levels of eviction and homelessness.

The findings will place greater pressure on the Government over housing policy following the Grenfell Tower fire disaster in west London, which exposed the neglect and disregard for people living in council-owned properties in one of the wealthiest areas of the capital.

The Shelter report highlights how a crisis of affordability and provision is gripping millions with no option but to look for homes in the private rented sector due to a shortage of social housing.

Shelter says that in 83% of areas of England, people in the private rented sector now face a substantial monthly shortfall between the housing benefit they receive and the cheapest rents, and that this will rise as austerity bites and the lack of properties tilts the balance more in favour of landlords.

Across the UK the charity has calculated that, if the housing benefit freeze remains in place as planned until 2020, more than a million households, including 375,000 with at least one person in work, could be forced out of their homes. It estimates that 211,000 households in which no one works because of disability could be forced to go.

Graeme Brown, the interim chief executive at Shelter, said: "The current freeze on housing benefit is pushing hundreds of thousands of private renters dangerously close to breaking point at a time when homelessness is rising."

A total of 14,420 households were accepted by local authorities as homeless between October and December 2016, up by more than half since 2009 – with 78% of the increase since 2011 being the result of people losing their previous private tenancy. Local authorities are under a legal obligation to find emergency accommodation, such as in bed and breakfasts.

In its report *Shut out: the barriers low-income households face in private renting*, to be published on Monday, Shelter calls for the freeze on the local housing allowance (paid to those renting privately) to be lifted immediately. The same demand has also been made by the Local Government Association, the Joseph Rowntree Foundation and the Chartered Institute of Housing.

While the Conservatives are under pressure to ease back on austerity (including the caps on benefits and public sector pay)Theresa May has said nothing to indicate she would end the housing benefits freeze. Labour has suggested it would do so as part of a £10-billion plan to inject greater fairness into the system.

"There is an assumption in housing policy that the private rented sector will be the default tenure for those priced out of home ownership or unable to secure a social tenancy, but this is increasingly not working," it says. "As the social rented sector contracts, private housing may have replaced it as the main tenure for people in housing need. But the market's limitations mean that significant government intervention is needed if it is to play an expanded role in preventing homelessness and housing people on low incomes."

Shelter says landlords are becoming choosier about who they rent out properties to, with many refusing to take those in receipt of benefits. Delays in payment have made them more reluctant to take on people they cannot rely on to pay up promptly.

Other factors make it near-impossible for many on low incomes to find the

money to start a private tenancy. "The upfront cost of private renting prohibits low-income households from accessing the private rented sector and means that many are forced to borrow, starting a tenancy in debt," says Shelter.

"For households experiencing multiple moves, the repeated costs of fees, deposits and rent in advance can pull them further into debt. Our advice services tell us that private landlords are increasingly asking for guarantors, who can be difficult for low-income households to secure." London has seen some of biggest rent increases since 2011–12, with the cheapest average rents rising on average by 6% a year for one- and two-bedroom properties. In Bristol, average rents at the lowest end of the market have also risen 6% a year for one-beds and for two-beds. In Luton, one-bed and two-bed rents have increased by 5% annually.

Nationwide, the increase in rents is starkest for rooms in shared houses, with rents increasing by nearly 4% annually over the time period. In London, rents for rooms in shared houses saw annual increases of 7%. A review by the Smith Institute citing a council officer saying that rooms in the private rented sector that had previously been used to meet housing need were now being rented out to young professionals who were able to pay the far higher rents.

By December 2016, nearly 76,000 households were living in emergency temporary accommodation such as bed and breakfasts, of which 60,000 were families with children or pregnant mothers. This is more than 10% up on the previous year and 58% more than in 2010 when just over 48,000 households were living in temporary accommodation.

24 June 2017

⇨ The above information is reprinted with kind permission from *The Guardian*. Please visit www.theguardian.com for further information.

Toxic housing crisis fuels a 700% rise in families forced to live in B&Bs – here's one mother's story

"Ministers should hang their heads in shame."

By Owen Bennett

Looking after an eight-month-old baby is a challenge for anyone, but Dian Walker is finding it tougher than most.

The mother-of-two was made homeless six weeks ago after falling behind with her rent, and now lives in a single room in a bed-and-breakfast with her baby and 11-year-old son.

The family has to share a bathroom with others in the B&B, including another family, which has two teenage children.

It is a far from ideal way to raise a family, especially as Dian's son – who does not want to be named – now has to travel from Ilford in east London to Edmonton in the north of the capital for school.

The Sainsbury's employee – who works part-time in customer service for the supermarket chain – is worried what the impact of the family's cramped living conditions are having on her children, particularly her eldest.

"He doesn't really like it," the 33-year-old told HuffPost UK.

"It's very uncomfortable. Sometimes he doesn't want to go back there. I keep telling him that things will get better soon. Sometimes he thinks this has happened because it's his fault."

Dian fell behind on her rent when she was on maternity leave after splitting from her new-born baby's father.

She owed her landlord more than £5,000 and was kicked out onto the streets.

Her attempts to find a new home in the private sector have been fruitless, as landlord after landlord refused to accept her housing benefit as payment.

"I can't afford to go back private. If I could, I wouldn't be in this situation," she said.

"It's not just the rent, it's finding a month's rent up-front, and a deposit and then letting fees."

Dian was placed in temporary accommodation by Waltham Forest Council, but instead of keeping her in the part of Greater London where her son goes to school, she was placed into a B&B in Ilford.

Her son now faces a commute to school along the busy North Circular Road, a journey Dian does not believe an 11-year-old should be making alone – meaning she has to accompany him every day.

This has placed question marks over whether she can return to work next month – something which will further exacerbate her financial woes.

Dian said: "It's so stressful. I do work, I try to do everything properly, but I have to provide so much information – bank statements going back two years – to prove to the council I deserve a proper place to live."

She added: "It's not easy because I have been depressed, I have been to counselling, but I have to stay strong."

Unfortunately, Dian's story is not unique – indeed, she is one of a growing number of people facing homelessness in the UK in 2017.

Government statistics reveal that since the Tories came to power in 2010, homelessness and the number of people living in temporary accommodation has risen dramatically.

In June 2010, the number of families with children living in B&Bs for more than six weeks was 160.

At the end of 2016, it was 1,260 – an increase of 688%.

When the figures include those who stay fewer than six weeks the increase is just as dramatic – a rise from 740 families with children in June 2010 to 2,780 in December 2016.

The total number of children in all kinds of temporary accommodation – B&Bs, hostels, women's refuges, council homes and private rooms – has increased from 72,590 to 118,960 over the same period.

Labour's Shadow Housing Secretary John Healey is damning his assessment of the Tories' record on the issue.

He said: "Ministers should hang their heads in shame that in a country as decent and well off as ours homelessness is rising. Under Conservative ministers the number of families without a permanent home has ballooned, and now includes almost 120,000 children.

"The hard truth for Tory ministers is that their decisions have caused this crisis: record low levels of new affordable rented housing, lack of action to help private renters and deep cuts to housing benefit and charity funding.

"It is now clear that after seven years of failure the Conservatives have no plan to fix the housing crisis.

"Labour in government would end rough sleeping, give renters new rights, and build thousands more affordable homes to rent and buy."

Housing charity Shelter, who is helping Dian get back onto her feet, called on whoever wins the election to get to grips with the housing crisis.

Anne Baxendale, director of communications, policy and campaigns at Shelter, said: "We have long been in the midst of a housing crisis in this country, with millions of ordinary people left to suffer the consequences of our failure to build enough affordable homes combined with cuts to welfare.

"But we don't have to accept the status quo and nor does the next government. Whoever wins in June will have the opportunity to fix the failures of the past by concentrating on building decent homes that people on lower incomes can realistically afford to live in. We look forward to working with them to achieve this."

12 May 2017

⇨ The above information is reprinted with kind permission from The Huffington Post UK. Please visit www.huffingtonpost.co.uk for further information.

If you thought the housing crisis was bad enough, the UK just lost its biggest funder of social housing

The £ billion given by European Investment Bank to UK social housing projects last year makes it the sector's biggest investor. This week it was confirmed that this investment would stop.

By Neena Gill

I worked for housing associations throughout the 80s and 90s and one memory remains more vivid than any other. I was called out to visit a new client who told us he had been trying to relocate for the past three years.

After climbing a steep set of stairs, I reached his second floor apartment. The man welcomed me in and explained that he was severely disabled from the waist down. He was wheelchair bound, so he was forced to remain indoors for all but essential trips. There was no lift.

On the rare occasions that he left the apartment, he had to scramble downstairs, using only his arms for balance. As you can imagine, wrenching himself upstairs again on the way back up was almost impossible.

Due to a lack of suitable housing it was difficult, but we were finally able to relocate him to a ground-floor apartment. When I delivered the good news, he broke down, flooding the room with tears of appreciation.

I have never seen anyone so grateful to be given something which should always have been their right. No one living in the UK – the world's fifth largest economy – should have their dignity stripped from them like this.

Sadly, these stories have become more common over the past 20 years. Much has been written about the housing crisis, but there has been little action. In Birmingham, only 780 homes were built in 2016. This means that the city's population is growing five times faster than homes are being built, pushing house prices up across the West Midlands.

A general housing crisis puts enormous pressure on social housing. The most vulnerable are the first to be neglected and their human rights to adequate shelter are too often forgotten.

The looming spectre of Brexit looks set to make the problem even worse. The £1 billion given by European Investment Bank (EIB) to UK social housing projects last year makes it the sector's biggest investor.

This week – as a direct result of the triggering of Article 50 – it was confirmed that this investment would stop. With the social housing sector already strained, we cannot afford to lose £1 of funding, let alone £1 billion.

We need to find substitute funds to help stem the deepening of the social housing crisis, but this will not cure the problem. The solution requires more than just funding: we need legislative changes that encourage the development of at least 300,000 houses per year. I suggest two.

The first, explained convincingly in yesterday's *Financial Times*, is to change the 1961 Land Compensation Act to let local authorities buy land at the current use value. Currently when councils buy land to build more housing, they are obliged to pay a price which includes potential planning permissions. This inflates pricing, discouraging the building of homes and inflating the costs of those that do exist.

Secondly, we need to agree to reformulate outdated regulations on green-belt land. Much of the so-called 'greenbelt' land is hardly green at all. The phrase may conjure up images of idyllic parkland, home to beautiful wildlife, but the reality is that much of

it is low-grade scrubland, inaccessible to the public.

Within the M25 that circles greater London there are 110,000 hectares of green-belt land. If we built on just one quarter of this land, we could provide more than one million new homes.

It is easy to get lost in statistics when talking about our housing crisis, but the reality is that this is a human problem. For every home under the required 300,000 not built, a family, a couple, or a single person is left without a suitable place to live.

The housing crisis is one of the biggest causes of inequality in this country, but it is also one of the simplest to solve. We just need to build more houses.

24 August 2017

⇨ The above information is reprinted with kind permission from *The Independent*. Please visit www.independent.co.uk for further information.

Government announces ambitious plan to build the homes Britain needs

The Government has introduced bold new plans to fix the broken housing market and build more homes across England.

Sajid Javid sets out "ambitious proposals to help fix the housing market so that more ordinary working people from across the country can have the security of a decent place to live".

The Government has today (7 February 2017) introduced bold new plans to fix the broken housing market and build more homes across England.

Communities Secretary Sajid Javid says the current system isn't working and is one of the greatest barriers to progress in Britain today.

The reforms in a white paper published today sets out new measures to ensure the housing market works for everyone, including people on lower incomes, renters, disabled and older people by:

Getting the right homes built in the right places

Consulting on the principle of a new, standardised way of calculating housing demand to reflect current and future housing pressures. Every local area will need to produce a realistic plan and review it at least every five years.

Currently, 40% of local planning authorities do not have an up-to-date plan that meets the projected growth in households in their area. Fixing this will help make sure enough land is released for new homes to be built in the parts of the country where people want to live and work and ensure developments take heed of local people's wishes, while continuing

with maximum protections for the green belt.

Councils and developers will also be expected to use land more efficiently by avoiding building homes at low density and building higher where there is a shortage of land and in locations well served by public transport such as train stations.

Speeding up house building

Giving local authorities the tools to speed up house building as well as powers to make sure developers build homes on time. The Government will make it easier for councils to issue completion notices, shortening the timescales to require developers to start building within two years, not three, when planning permission is granted.

We will also require greater transparency and information from developers on their pace of delivery of new housing so councils can consider this when planning their local need. This will help address the serious and growing gap between the number of planning permissions granted and the number of new homes completed.

Diversifying the market

Action to help small independent builders enter the market given including through the £3-billion Home Building Fund. Currently around 60% of new homes are built by just ten companies.

The fund will help us to build more than 25,000 new homes this Parliament and up to 225,000 in the longer term by providing loans

for SME builders, custom builders, offsite construction and essential infrastructure, creating thousands of new jobs in the process.

Sajid Javid is highlighting research that shows it is difficult to get on the housing ladder, with the average house now costing eight times more than average earnings – an all-time record.

The proportion of people living in the expensive private rented sector has doubled since 2000 and that more than 2.2 million working households with below-average incomes spend a third or more of their disposable income on housing.

This means they have less money to spend on other things every month, including putting aside money for a deposit.

Communities Secretary Sajid Javid said:

"Walk down your local high street today and there's one sight you're almost certain to see. Young people, faces pressed against the estate agent's window, trying and failing to find a home they can afford. With prices continuing to sky rocket, if we don't act now, a whole generation could be left behind. We need to do better, and that means tackling the failures at every point in the system.

The housing market in this country is broken and the solution means building many more houses in the places that people want to live.

We are setting out ambitious proposals to help fix the housing market so that more ordinary working people from across the country can have the security of a decent place to live. The only way to halt the decline in affordability and help more people onto the housing ladder is to build more homes. Let's get Britain building."

Housing Minister, Gavin Barwell said:

"We are setting out lasting reforms that will get more of the right homes built in the right places, right now.

We owe it to our children and our grandchildren to fix the broken housing market problems and help them find a home of their own."

Further measures in the housing white paper 'Fixing our broken housing market' include:

Homeowners

We have already helped more than 360,000 people buy through government-backed home-ownership schemes since 2010; helping people save for a deposit, buy with a smaller deposit, buy at 20% below the market price, buy the home they are renting from a social landlord, buy a share of a home or save a deposit while paying a below market rent.

Now in April 2017, the Government will introduce the Lifetime ISA. This will support younger adults to save flexibly for the long term, giving them a 25% bonus on up to £4,000 of savings a year. Savings and the bonus can be put towards the purchase of a first home, or withdrawn once they reach the age of 60.

Starter homes will be targeted at first-time buyers who would otherwise be priced out of the market. We intend to make clear through the National Planning Policy Framework that starter homes like shared ownership homes, should be available to households that need them most, with an income of less than £80,000 (£90,000 for London). The result of these changes means we will change our focus from starter homes to a wider range of affordable housing.

The wider range of government programmes will help over 200,000 people become homeowners by the end of the Parliament.

Affordable Rent and Rent to Buy

The Government is committed to building more affordable homes to boost house-building and support households who are locked out of the market.

At Autumn Statement we announced an extra £1.4 billion for our Affordable Homes Programme, taking total investment in this programme to over £7 billion to build around 225,000 affordable homes in this Parliament.

This investment will help families to find a decent home that is right for them. The 2016 to 2021 Affordable Homes Programme was originally designed to focus on delivering shared ownership. Now we have opened up the programme, relaxing restrictions on funding so providers can build a range of homes including for affordable rent.

This includes Rent to Buy homes alongside shared ownership, which will enable thousands of households to access home ownership through a product that fits their circumstances. Rent to Buy will help hard-working households to benefit from a discounted rent set flexibly at levels to make it locally affordable so they can save for a deposit to purchase their home.

Renters

The Government will put measures to tackle the high cost of renting at the heart of its plan to fix the broken housing market.

This includes amending planning rules so councils can proactively plan for more long-term Build to Rent homes and a consultation has been launched to allow developers to offer more affordable rent alongside other forms of affordable housing. Also ensuring more longer-term tenancies are available in private rented schemes to provide more stability to families renting.

We are working closely with the

British Property Federation and National Housing Federation to ensure that these longer tenancies become widely available

Green belt

Ministers have reaffirmed the Government's commitment to the green belt – that only in exceptional circumstances may councils alter green-belt boundaries after consulting local people and submitting the revised Local Plan for examination, and set out for the first time all the actions local authorities must take before considering the green belt.

The plan for 'Urban Regeneration' includes: strengthening national planning policy to create a de facto presumption in favour of housing on suitable brownfield land and to drive up density levels in high demand areas while ensuring that developments are well-designed and respect the character of the local area.

Also taking action to radically increase brownfield development and to bring life back to abandoned sites. That means high quality housing for families in town centres, breathing new life back into our high streets, turning abandoned shopping centres into new communities and increasing density of housing around transport hubs to build homes that people want to live in.

Empty homes

We will also continue to support local authorities to encourage efficient use of our existing stock, making best use of homes that are long-term empty.

Local authorities have powers and incentives to tackle empty homes. Through the New Homes Bonus they earn the same financial reward for bringing an empty home back into use as building a new one. They also have flexibility to impose a Council Tax premium of up to 50% (on top of the Council Tax bill), on properties that have been empty and substantially unfurnished for more than two years.

Great progress has been made in recent years and the number of empty homes stands at its lowest since records began. At May 2010, over 300,000 homes in England had been standing empty for longer than six months. As of October 2015 the number of long-term empty properties had fallen to 203,596.

Leasehold

The Government will act to promote fairness and transparency for the growing number of leaseholders.

Some buyers are not aware that buying a leasehold house can be more expensive than a freehold house in the long run. Some ground rents can increase significantly over the lease period and be traded, with leaseholders left in the dark. We will therefore consult on a range of measures to tackle all unfair and unreasonable abuses of leasehold.

Further support to help households who are currently priced out of the housing market to save for a deposit, and to buy or rent a home of their own. We will introduce a new Lifetime ISA in 2017, extend the Right to Buy discounts to housing association tenants, and invest in new homes for Shared Ownership, Affordable Rent and Rent to Buy.

7 February 2017

⇨ The above information is reprinted with kind permission from GOV.UK.

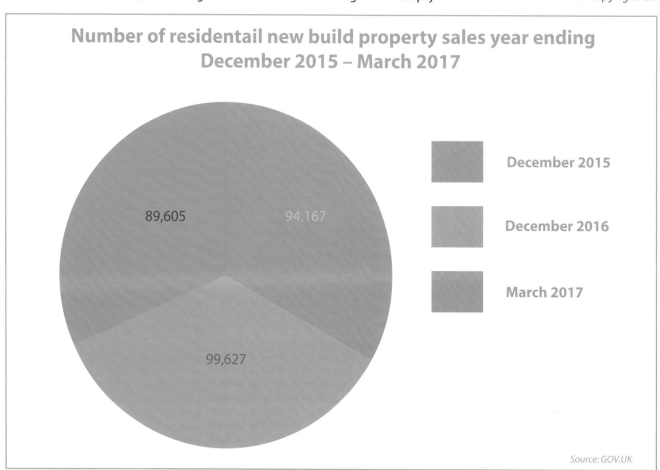

Number of residentail new build property sales year ending December 2015 – March 2017

89,605

94,167

99,627

December 2015

December 2016

March 2017

Source: GOV.UK

The future of housing and home: scenarios for 2030

The situation today

Housing has complex dynamics, but we can identify a number of key features which shape the current crisis. Critically, there aren't enough homes: a decade ago the Barker Review noted that around 250,000 homes needed to be built or made available every year to prevent a shortage of affordable homes and spiralling house prices. This target has been missed consistently, which has contributed to house prices becoming increasingly unaffordable. In England the average house price in 2014 was more than seven times the average salary. In a paper written ten years after her landmark review, Kate Barker wrote, "The chronic undersupply of new housing has led to a widespread housing affordability problem, and contributed to high market volatility in rising markets. This in turn generates growing inequality between those who own homes and those who cannot afford to." The think tank ResPublica observed in its Key Cities report that: "The provision of affordable housing is an issue affecting people in most parts of the country and one that continues to inhibit economic development." In the London Review of Books, James Meek was starker: "A housing shortage that has been building up for the past 30 years is reaching the point of crisis."

The younger generations struggle to buy a home. Currently, almost half of 25– 34-year-olds are renting privately, up from 21% in 2003–04. It's projected that in ten years' time only 39% of current 25-year-olds are likely to be buying their own home. In sharp contrast, almost two-thirds of those born in 1960 or 1970 were likely to be buying or own their own home by the age of 35, and 44% of those born in 1980. Housing tenure is changing fundamentally. The share of households owning or buying their own homes peaked in 2003, and there has been a 25-year decline in the proportion of people buying their own homes through a mortgage – there are now fewer of these than outright owners. Meanwhile, the proportion of private renters has reached the same levels as in the early 1970s, and has overtaken the number of social renters. On average, private rented households in the UK spend 39% of their income on paying their rent, compared to a European average of 28%.

People experiencing hardship or poverty are more likely to be living in private rented accommodation as a result of the rapid growth in the sector, rather than the social rented sector. Over the last 15 years rents have risen significantly faster than earnings, whilst government support has not kept pace. As the Institute of Fiscal Studies noted, since the mid-2000s "recent governments have responded to increases in HB expenditure by reducing the generosity of the benefit, often by weakening the link between entitlements and claimants' actual housing costs".

As the consequences of the housing crisis become increasingly stark, people are becoming more aware that the lack of affordable homes is a major problem for Britain. Nearly three-quarters of Britons (73%) believe that a lack of affordable housing is one of the biggest issues affecting the country. Almost three-fifths (58%) agree that "it is important to build lots of new houses to keep pace with growing demand". The British Social Attitudes Survey found in 2015 that the proportion of those in favour of house building in their area had climbed to 56%, up from 28% in 2010.

It is not simply a numbers game, however: people think new homes are too small, inside and out, characterless and of poorer build quality, although they identify that maintenance and energy costs are lower. In other words, they believe that newly built homes don't provide two of the top three things they are looking for when moving home: sufficient space in terms of both rooms and garden.

Towards 2030: the drivers of change

As we move from the present and the immediate past, there is also a set of long trends that frame the future. Each of the possible futures represented by the scenarios in this report is shaped to some extent by underlying factors that change slowly and are common to all scenarios. These both create an envelope within which the future will fold and also create opportunities for disruptive change from innovators who can break through the 'dilemmas of change' by reframing issues or reconnecting them in different ways. The nine drivers of change that follow here can be thought of as futures contexts.

1 Population growth

The population of both the UK and England is projected to increase. According to the Office of National Statistics' main projection, the population of the UK will grow by eight million, to 72 million in 2032, from 64 million in 2012. Almost all of that anticipated growth is in England, where population is projected to increase to 61 million from 54 million. The significant elements of this increase are a combination of fertility and longevity, and migration. At the same time, household size is falling, which exacerbates the issue.

2 Ageing

The population is ageing. The fastest-growing age cohort between 2012 and 2032 is the over-75s, who are projected by the ONS to grow by 3.5 million to 8.5 million, followed by the 60–74 age group, projected to grow by 2.9 million to 12.3 million. This is likely to have a disproportionate effect on housing demand, unless social trends change, because older people are more likely to live alone and are also more likely to live in a house with more bedrooms than they need. One potential resolution includes the development of 'care-ready' homes, which enable supported living for longer.

3 Slow economic growth

UK economic growth has been weak since the financial crisis.

Jobs growth has not been matched by increases in wages, productivity, or business investment. All taken together, this suggests that lower than trend economic growth is likely to continue into the future. Economists also believe that we may be seeing an international period of 'secular stagnation', in which lower growth is widespread. Indeed, the OECD projects that long trends in the global economy mean that global economic growth will be slower across the next half-century. There are consequences for household spending choices, which would be constrained, and potentially for government willingness to invest.

4 Persistent levels of poverty

Levels of poverty in the UK increased sharply during the 1980s, and have remained at higher levels since. Using the guideline of people with incomes below 60% of median income levels, the proportion of individuals below the poverty line has remained above 20% for most of the last two decades. This includes households in work, and indicates relatively high levels of child poverty. In the past, policy attempts to reduce this – even with significant political commitment – have had only modest effects, so it seems likely that this will be a persistent feature of the UK social and economic landscape, with consequences for housing provision.

5 Maturing of the digital technology sector

The rate at which new digital users come online in the UK has slowed significantly. But at the same time there has been a sharp increase in people who mainly access the Internet from mobile devices: two-thirds of UK adults, or 95% of smartphone users, now access the Internet from mobile phones. 87% of British adults now access the Internet in some way, although the proportion is much lower among over-55s. At the same time there are continuing issues about online privacy, where regulation is likely to accelerate, and an increased use of passive sensors to monitor and manage.

6 Shifting values

In general, we are seeing a shift towards 'post-materialist' values, in which people value autonomy and diversity, and move away from authority and hierarchy. At the same time, the British Social Attitudes survey shows a steady hardening of attitudes towards welfare. But this picture is becoming more complex. Post-election research shows that while 45% of people (and 48% of voters) agreed that "People who work hard can get on in Britain" – as opposed to "The way our society and economy works stops people getting the opportunities they deserve" – only 36% of 18–34s shared this view. Without a steady improvement in the economy, this age differential seems likely to increase.

7 Regional bias towards London

The centralising pull of London, for investment (including infrastructure investment), wages and jobs, is a distinctive feature of the UK, with the effect that cities such as Manchester, Birmingham, Bristol and so on have less economic and political impact. In particular, most of the UK's large cities outside of London have lower than average growth rates and productivity levels. Martin, Gardiner and Tyler (2014) note, "On the basis of past trends, overall one might expect that for the next few years at least, many northern cities will either continue to fall further behind those in the south in relative wealth creation, productivity and job generation". It remains to be seen whether political will to reverse these trends is successful.

8 Increasing political fragmentation

The long-run trend towards party political fragmentation is continuing. At the last election, the three mainstream parties attracted 75% of the total vote, compared to 89% in 2010. This trend is common across Europe and goes back to the 1950s, so is unlikely to reverse, although the rate of decline is likely to be slower in forthcoming elections.

9 Skills and materials shortages in housebuilding sector

According to the Federation of Master Builders, skills shortages in the building sector worsened for every single skill category in 2014. In the last year of peak building, 2007–08, when the construction sector managed 200,000 homes, much of this gap was filled with migrant workers. The existing workforce is ageing, and new recruits are not coming into the industry sufficiently fast to replace them. There are also shortages of materials.

April 2016

⇨ The above information is reprinted with kind permission from Shelter. Please visit england.shelter.org.uk for further information.

Should Britain build on its green spaces to solve the housing crisis?

An article from **The Conversation.**

THE CONVERSATION

By Alister Scott, Professor of Environment and Spatial Planning, Northumbria University, Newcastle

Back in the 1930s, English planners came up with a novel idea to prevent urban sprawl: a ring of countryside surrounding the city, protected from development by law. This 'green belt' would preserve the unique characters of historic towns, safeguard the countryside from development and encourage the regeneration and reuse of urban land. It was adopted nationally in 1955, and around 13% of England is now zoned as green-belt land.

But today, the UK is experiencing a housing crisis. The nation requires 220,000 new homes each year to keep up with demand – not to mention making up for the undersupply from previous years. In the year to September 2016, only 141,000 were built. This deficit has sparked renewed debate over the value of the green belt.

Leading housebuilders and think tanks argue that selectively releasing parts of the green belt would help to meet the government's ambitious housebuilding targets. Meanwhile, other pressure groups claim that the green belt should be sacrosanct, to safeguard the environmental and health benefits it provides for nearby towns and cities.

Under threat?

In theory, the green belt is protected within the Government's planning framework. Alterations to the green-belt boundaries can only be made by local governments in exceptional circumstances, and individual planning applications on green belt sites are only approved under very special circumstances.

In practice, though, it seems the criteria aren't always quite so strict. Increasingly, greenfield sites (undeveloped land, which can include the green belt) are being favoured by developers because they are cheaper to exploit than brownfield sites (previously developed land, such as disused industrial estates), which have much higher transaction costs.

In fact, national planning policy encourages development on greenfield sites through the use of highly questionable 'objective' assessments (or rather, estimates) of housing need, based on past trends and dubious population projections. What's more, measures of economic viability only take stock of profit, and fail to incorporate environmental or social considerations.

The case for development is also propped up by overly simplified claims that much of the green belt is poor-quality, unproductive land, with no clear requirements for good management.

Hidden values

The incremental assaults on the green belt overlook the need for vital infrastructure and services to create strong, resilient communities and sustainable places. In fact, the green belt holds significant market and non-market value for urban economies, which pose a challenge conventional economic arguments in favour of more houses on 'unproductive' green-belt land.

For one thing, releasing the green belt in the wrong place comes with certain costs, such as longer commutes, worse congestion and more dangerous levels of air pollution, as well as increased risk of surface water flooding. These costs are normally exacted after development, and don't appear in initial assessments.

The green belt when seen as part of critical green infrastructure has the potential to deliver multiple benefits for cities: it provides space for agriculture, protection from flooding and drought, it improves air quality and mitigates the urban heat island effect, as well as enabling recreation and enhancing biodiversity.

Hatching a plan

The challenge, then, is to identify where these benefits of the green-

belt can be optimised, and the costs of development minimised. At a national level, England lacks a strategic plan to identify the best sites for housing, jobs and key infrastructure. This is needed to drive sustainable growth and address deep-rooted problems, such as the divide between the wealthy but congested south-east, and the less prosperous north.

On a local level, it means planning to put the right developments in the right place. This isn't limited to houses: city outskirts can be rejuvenated by community food-growing initiatives, or wetlands created for flood protection and biodiversity. Local authorities should think and plan strategically and form long-term visions about the kind of places they want to create – just like the great planners of England's historic garden cities.

The recent housing white paper requires local authorities to meet housing demand, but crucially fails to move away from fetish on housing numbers and address the current strategic planning void. It does, however, propose a standard method for calculating housing need, which is welcome and will prevent delays to local plans over disputed methodologies.

Strategic, cross-boundary planning can help to make the green belt more productive and deliver more houses. Green-belt value can be enhanced through positive management of its natural capital. It's time to leave behind the polarised and siloed green-belt debate, and recognise that housing, industry, transport, community, landscape and environment are vital pieces of the planning jigsaw for cities, towns and countryside.

7 February 2017

⇨ The above information is reprinted with kind permission from *The Conversation*. Please visit www. theconversation.com for further information.

Green-belt myths: what you need to know

Many reports focus on weakening green-belt protection to allow greater freedom for large housebuilders. However, the arguments within these reports are based on a highly selective reading of the evidence and give little consideration to the wide range of benefits provided by green-belt policy. They urgently need to be challenged.

Green-belt policy was established in 1955 primarily to stop urban sprawl. There are now 14 separate areas of green belt that cover 13% of England; mostly open land and countryside around the largest or most historic towns and cities. Campaign to Protect Rural England has campaigned for Green Belts since our formation in 1926. We remain a strong supporter of Green-belt policy, which aims to provide a permanently protected belt of open land through tight controls over certain forms of development.

The issue

The National Planning Policy Framework and the 2015 Conservative Manifesto stated clearly that Ministers attach great importance to the green belt and will maintain existing levels of protection. In March this year, the Prime Minister declared that protecting the green belt is "paramount".

Yet, there have been several reports, from bodies such as the Adam Smith Institute, Aecom and London First, calling for large-scale development in the green belt. The reports focus on weakening green belt protection to allow greater freedom for large housebuilders. They reflect the growing influence private sector consultancies, and others acting on behalf of large developers, are having in debates over planning issues – a trend highlighted last year by concerned academics. However, the arguments put forward by these reports need to be challenged.

Myth 1: Green-belt is an old fashioned idea and it's time to pension it off.

Why this is wrong: The benefits of green belt remain as vital as ever. By looking at other countries we can see that without the strong protection it offers against most forms of development, more valuable countryside would be consumed by urban sprawl – and the character of our towns and cities would be irreversibly eroded.

For 60 years, green belts have protected agricultural and other undeveloped land. By doing this they encourage the regeneration of previously developed or 'brownfield' land in urban areas. International comparisons suggest that without the strong protection green belts offer against many forms of development, much more farmland and woods would be consumed by urban sprawl, especially around large cities. Yet with the increasing global pressures from climate change and population growth, our farmland and woodlands will become more valuable in future, not less. The calls for more development in the green belt assume that this land is only valuable if built on, an assumption that is fundamentally flawed. The green belt is needed now more than ever.

Myth 2: Green belt is safe from development.

Why this is wrong: green belt is under a renewed and growing level of threat.

Sajid Javid, Secretary of State for Communities and Local Government, has stated in Parliament that the green belt is "absolutely sacrosanct." This has echoed the 2015 Conservative general election manifesto, which pledged to maintain green belt protection, and other previous statements by senior politicians. In March 2015 the former Prime Minister David Cameron claimed that "development on green belt is at its lowest rate since modern records began 25 years ago". But this statement is unlikely to remain true for much longer. Research carried out in June 2015 on behalf of BBC Radio 4's *File on 4* programme by Glenigan, a leading provider of construction data, found a sharp increase in the number of houses securing full planning approval in the green belt. In 2009/10, 2,258 homes were approved.

In 2013/2014, the number had risen to 5,607. By the following year, 2014/2015, it had more than doubled to 11,977.

CPRE analysis has found that existing and emerging local plans are proposing more than 362,000 houses on the green belt. As proposals in local plans are at an earlier stage in the pipeline than full planning approval, the vast majority, if not all, of these houses will be in addition to the figures mentioned by Glenigan. Ministers have taken action to address some of the most unnecessary local plan proposals. The Government now needs to act on the national imperative to protect the green belt by making clear that green belt land should only be developed in exceptional cases, and that economic growth is not in itself an 'exceptional case'.

Myth 3: Green-belt protection pushes house prices up.

Why this is wrong: much house price inflation is down to economic factors that increasingly treat houses as an investment opportunity rather than somewhere to live.

Suggestions that green belt policy is responsible for pushing up house prices are usually part of a wider critique of the planning system. It has been claimed that "a near theological protection of Green Belt land explains why millions of young people can't afford to buy a home." But if green belt affected house prices, then it would be more expensive, all things being equal, to buy a house in a city protected by green belt than one that is not. There is no evidence this is the case.

CPRE contends that the significant factors that stimulate housing demand well beyond the capacity of the market to supply it, and so drive up prices, actually include:

⇨ the control of the supply of land by major housebuilding companies and land speculators with new houses being trickled out in order to maximise sales returns;

⇨ the relatively poor performance of rival investments such as equities and pensions;

⇨ low interest rates, which make it easier to borrow more;

⇨ a wide range of strongly marketed mortgage products;

⇨ the growth in notional wealth tied up in people's houses, which has enabled many owners to enter the 'buy-to-let' market by borrowing against their current homes, or help their children to become home owners in the same way.

If we loosened green-belt controls or de-designated large areas of it, we would simply allow more land to be built on, where developers can make maximum profit, as has been the experience of other countries in Europe, particularly Ireland and Spain. There is plenty of other, more suitable land that could be built on, and it could be used more effectively. In 2014, a CPRE report found that there is enough suitable brownfield land, available now, for at least one million new homes. It also demonstrated that brownfield land is not a finite resource. It is constantly being replenished, and a CPRE analysis of new 'brownfield registers' produced by 53 local authorities in October 2016 found that 11% more housing could be provided on brownfield sites in those areas compared to 2014. Usually, many more homes are delivered on a brownfield site than an equivalent area of greenfield land. Government land use change statistics show that, in every year since 2004, we have consistently built on average 50% more houses on brownfield sites than on equivalent areas of greenfield. We should use this land before even considering going into the green belt.

Myth 4: Green belt has little or no environmental value.

Why this is wrong: the environmental value of individual parcels of green belt land is not the prime concern. Green belt's primary purpose is to prevent urban sprawl, but in doing so it provides countryside close to 30 million people. A huge proportion of it has considerable environmental value. In the face of climate change, it has an increasingly important role in storing carbon and preventing flooding and is a vital economic resource for food security and soil protection.

Two-thirds of all green-belt land is in agricultural use; not surprising given its proximity to potential markets in the city. This is a vital economic resource for food security and soil protection. Yet some green belt critics

claim the way it is farmed makes it worthless environmentally. The London School of Economics' Paul Cheshire argues: "The most important land use in green belts is intensive arable, which generates negative net environmental benefits," referencing the National Ecosystem Assessment of June 2011 in support of this.

It is disingenuous to argue that agricultural land has no positive environmental value, and especially to claim the National Ecosystem Assessment supports such an argument. In fact, the NEA recognises the huge value to society of agricultural land, both in terms of food production and in 'cultural services' (such as the sense of well-being produced by seeing an agricultural landscape). The NEA also notes that biodiversity and some landscape features (particularly hedgerows) have declined in many agricultural landscapes but emphasises that this trend has begun to reverse through better land management.

Away from benefits of the agricultural land, green belts provide countryside close to 30 million people, giving us 29,000 km of public rights of way, 68,000 ha of Sites of Special Scientific Interest (SSSIs) and just under 140,000 ha of deciduous woodland. In particular, England's green belts contain 34% of our local nature reserves and 17% of our ancient woodland, a relatively higher proportion than countryside without the Green Belt designation. 48 new Local Nature Reserves have been created in the green belt since 2009, 30% of the total of all new LNRs created in England. In the face of climate change, the green belt is also likely to have an increasingly significant role in storing carbon and preventing flooding.

The protection against development afforded by the green belt designation has often played a critical role in increasing the environmental benefits of land covered by the policy. To give two examples, the New Forest became a National Park in 2006 after green-belt policy helped keep the area largely free of development over a number of decades. Also, Windsor Great Park (within the Metropolitan Green Belt) has been

valued by the Government's Natural Capital Committee (NCC) as having environmental benefits worth at least £49 million, or £7,600 per hectare. Allowing development on land that is poor will only encourage landowners to neglect it. In April 2015, leading environmental economist and Chair of the NCC, Dieter Helm, published a paper seeking to challenge many of the arguments for green belt deregulation put forward by developers and other economists. As Helm argues, where the quality of Green Belt land is poor, the solution is to improve it. For example, the Community Forests initiative has turned more than 20,000 hectares of often degraded green belt land into woodland or other natural habitats since 1990.

By contrast, the analysis of the value of green belts by the Adam Smith Institute relies on a single study of land near Chester from 1992, suggesting that green belt land provided environmental benefits to society worth £889 per hectare. The comparison with the NCC's more recent valuation of Windsor Great Park shows that extrapolating a 23-year-old study from a single location will not give a reliable picture of the true current value – let alone the potential value – of the green belt overall.

Myth 5: Green belts only benefit people who own property within them rather than the wider public.

Why this is wrong: preventing sprawl, one of the key purposes of green belt policy, produces financial benefits to society by reducing the infrastructure and environmental costs associated with new development. This claim also ignores the vast number of people on low incomes who live in towns and villages surrounded by green belt and enjoy its benefits.

Green belt policy is designed to prevent sprawl and all the negative costs associated with it. A recent research report from the London School of Economics found that urban sprawl in the USA imposes costs to society as a whole of more than $1 trillion. This report shows that the costs of sprawl fall into two significant categories:

The loss of undeveloped land and all the services that this provides, particularly in relation to food production and reduced ecological services.

More dispersed activity, including reduced accessibility, higher costs of public infrastructure and longer trip distances. (This issue is discussed further under Myths 6 and 7 below.)

Green-belt land is part of the wider countryside, to which there were 1.3 billion visits in 2013–14, according to government surveys. A 2016 survey, using samples from the same programme, found that 40% wanted to visit the green belt more often for woodland walks, and 32% wanted more nature reserves. Education was the other favoured option, with 27% wanting more educational visits such as to farms. The green belt is already used regularly by local ramblers groups, the Guides and Scouts, Duke of Edinburgh Award Scheme participants, local schools, and many others, with no restrictions on grounds of class or income.

Myth 6: Just building on a small proportion of green belt would leave us with more than enough.

Why this is wrong: much of the integrity and therefore benefits of green belt would be lost if we did this, including preventing sprawl, and towns joining up.

Releasing just a small percentage of green belt sounds an attractive way of releasing land for housing. But once bits of the green belt are removed, the integrity is reduced and so its benefits begin to be lost. Permanence is also an important feature of green belt so people, businesses and the Government (through supporting environmentally sensitive farming on green-belt land) have had the confidence to invest in the area on that basis. Conversely, the temptation is removed for people to buy green-belt land in the hope that it will be de-designated and its notional value for development will increase.

It has been claimed that: "You can build one million new homes on 3.7% of the green belt (or 2.5 million homes on just over 60,000 ha of green belt) within walking distance of a train station.' This, and other claims like it, are often presented as a more moderate alternative to abolishing green belt policy outright. But closer analysis shows that, in many areas, they would have much the same effect, defeating the key purposes of preventing sprawl and stopping places joining up with each other. For example, Potters Bar, Slough, and Watford would all end up becoming part of London. The green belt would also become less accessible to people travelling by rail from the urban area it embraces.

Myth 7: If we don't allow development in the green belt, people will leapfrog it and commute in an unsustainable fashion from elsewhere.

Why this is wrong: we need to be creating jobs near where people live or enable them to work across distance, rather than encouraging long commutes. However, commuting from beyond the green belt can be sustainable if there are fast public transport links available.

Building in the green belt is not a solution to unsustainable commuting. On the contrary, it would lead to more people leapfrogging over the suburbs into city centres. There are strong reasons to believe that large scale development might actually encourage more car-based commuting in particular. Analysis of 2011 Census

data by the Royal Town Planning Institute (RTPI) found that in five towns in Berkshire and Hertfordshire surrounded by the Metropolitan Green Belt, 72% of commuters travelled by private vehicle and only 7.4% commuted to London by train. For each new house built in the green belt, the report estimated, between four and seven additional car trips per week could be generated. Instead, we need to do more to create jobs near where people live rather than far away from housing they can afford.

In large, buoyant cities such as London, there is a particular need for more affordable housing within the inner city. Also, our biggest cities aren't the only places where jobs can be and are being created. The Centre for Cities found that Milton Keynes increased employment rates by 18% between 2004 and 2013, creating new jobs faster than any other town in the country. Other high performers included Hastings and Portsmouth – both places with plenty of brownfield land available for regeneration.

Alternatively, people need the tools to be able to work remotely when they choose to do so. The growth of digital technologies reduces the impact of distance and allows appropriately skilled people to offer services from virtually any location in the country, provided there is a fast broadband connection. The digital sector is seen as a key area in which England's

economy is expected to expand in the coming years, and this economic development is already appearing in new digital economy clusters across the country. A recent report found 74% of digital companies are based outside London, including places such as Hull, Liverpool and the north east.

'Leapfrogging' is also not inherently unsustainable if a good transport network exists. Dieter Helm argues that "transport is not about the distance in miles, but rather the speed of connecting links" (between homes and workplaces). Green belt critics often cite transport problems in historic towns surrounded by green belt such as Bath, Cambridge, and Oxford. But in these cases the green belt for the most part extends no further than ten miles beyond the urban edge (and in many instances over a far smaller distance), and thereby adds little in itself to journey distances. Problems with the transport network in these and other areas are far better explained by an over-reliance on car travel, and conversely the often poor quality of public transport, rather than by the presence of the green belt.

Myth 8: Green belts have the effect of confining the urban poor to live at high densities in the cities.

Why this is wrong: all cities have areas of urban poor, whether or not they have green belts. There is a great need now for new affordable housing, but growing inequalities between rich and poor are a global phenomenon that cannot realistically be blamed on the use of green belts in England.

Green belts were established in government policy in 1955 and then were gradually designated in Local Plans, alongside programmes of urban slum clearance and dispersal to new or expanded towns within or beyond the green belts. Many of these places, such as Milton Keynes, Peterborough and Swindon, have large populations of people on average or below average household incomes, but the overall population density in these and other English towns and cities is around average, and often quite low, compared with other cities in the European Union. The idea that post-war English planning policies have

somehow 'confined' the poor is not supported by the evidence.

There is a great need now to improve access to housing for those who cannot afford to buy on the open market. Much more affordable housing needs to be built. But growing inequalities between rich and poor in this and other respects are a global phenomenon that cannot realistically be blamed on the use of green belt policy in England. Some commentators have attempted to suggest a causal link with "growing housing demand in the postwar period" by referring to the doubling of the designated area of green belt since 1978. This is a distortion of the truth and a tenuous claim.

As CPRE and Natural England point out, the doubling in area since 1978 is in the area of formally designated green belts. The green belts had largely been agreed in principle as early as the 1950s, and large-scale New Town development and other housebuilding for the council and social sectors took place alongside this until well into the 1980s. Housebuilding has declined since the 1980s due to the end of large-scale housebuilding by the public sector, rather than because of the formal designation of green belt land.

Myth 9: Green-belt policy leads to more land being used for golf courses than new housing.

Why this is wrong: the housing definition used in this argument ignores gardens and access roads – and why shouldn't people use green-belt land for outdoor recreation?

Green belts are, by definition, areas where new housing development is strictly controlled. Commentators refer to wider problems with a relative lack of new housing (see also Myths 3 and 8 above). Green-belt critics often draw a comparison between the amount of England's land area taken up for golf courses and that taken for new housing. These comparisons are misleading because they usually make a considerable underestimate of the amount of land taken up by housing.

A BBC Radio 4 *More Or Less* programme, broadcast on 30 May 2014, explored the argument that more of Surrey's land area (2.8%) is taken up by golf courses than housing (2.1%). Most land outside urban areas in Surrey is classified as green belt. As the programme went on to highlight, the figures quoted for land area of housing do not include gardens, or access roads. If these are added, then about 14% of Surrey's area is taken up by housing. Nationally, more than five times more land is used for housing when gardens and roads are included, than for golf courses.

A wide range of leisure activities take place in the green belt, not only golf but also horse riding and other outdoor sports. These all reflect in some way the value of a belt of open land to the people in the urban areas the land surrounds.

Myth 10: Green belt stops any kind of development or beneficial land management at all so land is abandoned and neglected.

Why this is wrong: green belt does not restrict development connected with agriculture, forestry or public infrastructure. Neglect is less of a problem in the green belt than in the countryside as a whole.

Green-belt policy restricts housebuilding, but allows many forms of so-called "appropriate development" to take place, especially in relation to agriculture, forestry, outdoor recreation and public infrastructure such as reservoirs, cemeteries and sewage works. Conversely, local authorities can also use planning powers to improve the environmental condition of undeveloped land, both within and outside the green belt. If green belt designation was linked to the quality of land management, there would be an active incentive to run land down to justify taking it out of the green belt. Landowners would also seek a much higher price for the land in the hope of later being able to sell it for housing development.

Surveys by Natural England in 2009 found that the quality of the landscape is being maintained on more than twice as much green belt land (39%) as where it's neglected (18%). In fact, green belt has a lower proportion of land classed as "neglected" than the national average, while just 0.2% of it is described as "derelict".

August 2015

⇨ The above information is reprinted with kind permission from the Campaign to Protect Rural England. Please visit www.cpre.org.uk for further information.

© Campaign to Protect Rural England 2017

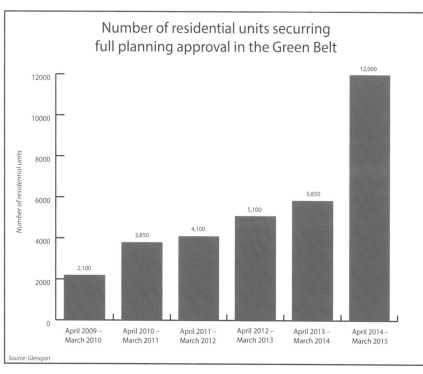

Number of residential units securing full planning approval in the Green Belt

- April 2009 – March 2010: 2,100
- April 2010 – March 2011: 3,850
- April 2011 – March 2012: 4,100
- April 2012 – March 2013: 5,100
- April 2013 – March 2014: 5,850
- April 2014 – March 2015: 12,000

Number of residential units

Source: Glenigan

Keeping it sustainable: how intelligent data revitalises brownfield sites

According to the Office for National Statistics, just over 65 million people reside in the UK. England is the most populous nation with 54 million people, most of whom live in urban neighbourhoods. The commercial property market is also very strong in metropolitan areas. While some businesses opt for an 'out-of-town' base to reduce operating costs, city centres remain preferred locations.

The trend for urban expansion has been acknowledged by both central and local government. The Department for Communities and Local Government's Housing White Paper stresses that the country must make as much use as possible of previously developed 'brownfield' land for homes – "so that this resource is put to productive use, to support the regeneration of our cities, towns and villages, to support economic growth and to limit the pressure on the countryside".

Brownfield development is better business for infrastructure professionals

The perception and value of these brownfield projects became the talk of the construction sector with the introduction of the development of the Olympic Park and Village, a programme of works carried out over a nine-year period to 2012 which injected an initial £9.9 billion into the British economy.

Infrastructure development created 8,000 subcontracting jobs.

By 2014, this figure was £14 billion and investment in the development (estimated at just over £17bn) had almost reached an equal cost to benefit ratio.

Centrepiece of a new build infrastructure network

The Olympic Park and Village were entirely constructed on brownfield land in east London. In previous years, the site had been used for industrial purposes and among the major considerations were the level of toxicity in the soil, disused water and gas mains, historic railway and electrical lines as well as the requirement for compulsory purchase orders.

These items were just some on a tick list of scores of considerations for the Olympics project's master planners. Concepts for the complex project became symbolic of the UK's innovative capability in planning, construction, engineering and infrastructure.

According to the London Legacy Development Corporation, some of the architectural structures that are now part of this new community are the ArcelorMittal Orbit (tipped for further development), Copper Box Arena, Lee Valley Hockey and Tennis Centre, Lee Valley VeloPark, London Aquatics Centre and the Olympic Stadium.

The world's most complex round of 'I-spy'

The development of a new residential area (with 2,800 homes built by the end of 2014) was designed to be an example of a 'green infrastructure' environment. This meant the creation of an eco-friendly landscape and sustainable structures together with a full infrastructure delivery programme of new roads, railway expansion, telecommunications, gas and electricity.

Before a single hectare of ground could be broken, the thousands of professionals contracted to transform the site from concept to reality relied on intelligent data to confirm the location of disused elements of previous infrastructure networks below the landscape.

Data-driven regeneration is the new standard

The land remediation project for 2012 used building information modelling (BIM) across the project within the framework of best practice in spatial data infrastructure to facilitate information exchange.

By 2015, the Olympic legacy had further progressed to the Stratford Waterfront development project which is now being touted as an 'Olympicopolis'. The approximate value to the local economy when completed is £2.8 billion. The total stake in the project is £1.3 billion and is representative of combined public and private sector investment. Every element of the project and projects of its kind across the globe are reliant on data-driven technology.

This is an exciting time for businesses involved in infrastructure planning and for aspiring professionals. Land Registry holds detailed ownership and extent information for all property registered in England and Wales. To learn more about how the application of spatial data can offer improved insight to support your next project visit us online now. If you're new to the infrastructure sector, please keep up with our blog series.

9 February 2017

⇨ The above information is reprinted with kind permission from HM Land Registry. Please visit blog. landregistry.gov.uk for further information.

Tiny houses: the big idea that could take some heat out of the housing crisis

An article from The Conversation.

THE CONVERSATION

By Robert Kronenburg, Roscoe Professor of Architecture, University of Liverpool

If you could have a new home, exactly to your specification for about a year's average salary wouldn't you take it? Many people, in the US, UK and Europe want to find an alternative housing solution that is cheap and mortgage free but also ecologically sustainable. The solution may be to build so-called "tiny houses" – very small dwellings, often built on trailers, that make the most of unused, unwanted or free sites in the city or country.

The tiny house is, indeed, tiny. It comes in at less than 25 square metres, but is able to provide comfort and security at minimum cost. These are primarily wooden buildings and can be bought ready-to-use or can be assembled by their future occupant. For as little as £15,000, you can buy a kit, or for up to £50,000 you can get a fully assembled and fitted-out home for two.

Because of their size they can be built on a steel-framed base similar to a trailer or caravan, meaning they can be mobile and therefore capable of use on temporary sites. They are usually single-space dwellings, sometimes with an open loft for sleeping reached by a ladder or steep stair with a shower room below. Most people would choose to set up a permanent or temporary connection to conventional services, but you can also go off-grid with solar panels, wood burners and bottled gas for energy needs, and chemical toilets or outhouses for sanitation.

Cutting back

There are now so many tiny house enthusiasts that it can justifiably be described as a movement, with online forums for practised and aspiring builders to share ideas and experiences. These houses are both cute and eccentric. Perhaps they tap into a common aspiration that people had as children to build a fort, a tree house or a den. However, they also meet the deep human need to find a home that is just right for us. For those who have built their own tiny house there is a special sense of connection to something made by their own hand, tuned to their own needs, even if they have used other people's plans and commercially available components.

Tiny house advocates are attracted for both practical and cultural reasons. Although the idea of sorting out your main living expense for the price of a family car is undoubtedly a key motivation, it is also about empowerment of the individual to step outside the corporate idea that "bigger and more expensive is better". Tiny house owners no longer aspire to an island kitchen unit or a wide screen TV in the basement, and it's fair to say that buying stuff slows right down when you have nowhere to put it.

It is also about environmental responsibility and sustainable living. These buildings, simply because of their size, use considerably less energy both in their construction and running costs. The inclusion of other simple efficiencies such as LED lighting, super-insulation and water reclamation simultaneously boosts ecological credibility and lowers monthly bills.

A sustainable life

We might think that this sort of living stems from ultra-modern, post-capitalist thinking, but in truth, it isn't a new concept. The historic roots of the tiny house movement are in the traditional buildings that 17th-century settlers first built when homesteading North America and before that in earlier European rural precedents. These were simple, often one-room buildings, built on minimal stone foundations and made from local timber hewn to shape.

The modern versions are often built to the same or better construction standard as full-size houses, but contemporary American tiny house owners relate to the early settlers' way of life using minimal resources, and to Henry David Thoreau's

book Walden: *A Life in the Woods*, an important and influential record of the author's experiment to live a sustainable life.

However, there are hurdles to overcome in tiny house living. A major issue is identifying suitable and available sites. In both Europe and North America planning legislation is clearly aimed at conventional buildings with expensive, long-term connections to services such as water supply, drainage, electricity and gas. Obtaining permission to set up a tiny house in an urban area close to employment and resources isn't easy.

In the UK, the problem can be even more difficult with planning permission hard to obtain unless the building type meets recognised size, type and materials guidelines. The mobility aspect of many tiny houses can be a bonus here as in theory it enables owners to take advantage of temporary sites with the capacity to relocate when permission expires, or their requirements change.

The crucial question, of course, is whether the tiny house helps solve the larger housing problem in the UK, where housing charity Shelter estimates 250,000 dwellings are needed each year. It is a possibility if planning restrictions on dwelling size and typology can be relaxed and construction companies are willing to take on such low- cost work on the small sites these buildings can utilise. However, a fundamental problem of providing any affordable accommodation in property hotpots would also need to be addressed by government legislation, ensuring these desirable little residences were only occupied by their owners and not gobbled up by absentee investors.

9 March 2017

⇨ The above information is reprinted with kind permission from *The Conversation*. Please visit www.theconversation.com for further information.

The importance of building zero-carbon homes

Steve Hornblow sets out some of the thinking behind the initiatives deployed at the first phase of the NW Bicester development, ensuring homes meet true zero-carbon status.

NW Bicester is the UK's first eco town that will create up to 6,000 new true zero-carbon homes; pioneering the highest standards in sustainable construction that can be enjoyed for generations to come.

2016 marked the delivery of 91 homes in phase one of the 'Elmsbrook' development at NW Bicester which, when complete, will comprise 393 highly energy efficient homes in total, and a local centre with 40% green space.

The new homes were launched in 2015 through the FABRICA by A2Dominion brand, with the initial residents moving in April 2016. Built with zero waste to landfill during construction, Elmsbrook is the first true zero-carbon development of its size in the UK and is one of only 16 communities worldwide to have been awarded Bioregional's One Planet Community status.

The design and materials used on all of the properties at Elmsbrook ensure the homes are future proofed for climate change up to 2050 with features such as triple glazed windows that can have exterior blinds retro-fitted to reduce solar gain associated with global temperature rises, and rainwater harvesting to help reduce water consumption from 150 litres to 80 litres per person per day.

Exemplary energy efficiency is key to the design of the true zero-carbon homes and includes solar PVs on every roof, a Combined Heat and Power (CHP) Energy Centre with district heating network providing heat and hot water to all homes, and real-time energy monitoring and travel information via a tablet information system (Shimmy) in every home.

As residents have moved in, a number of sustainable transport initiatives have been launched to benefit the new true zero-carbon community and support A2Dominion's wider vision to reduce the number of local journeys made by petrol or diesel cars from the current Bicester average of 67.5% to 50% by 2026.

As well as appointing a dedicated travel plan co-ordinator for Elmsbrook, A2Dominion has worked closely with local Bicester family firm, Grayline Coaches, to launch a new, bespoke, low emissions zone compliant bus service from the development from first occupations. The service is also accessible to existing Bicester residents.

A2Dominion has partnered with the E Car Club to launch an electric car hire service, which is the first in Bicester.

The vehicles are available any time to all residents from £4.50 per hour including hire, power and insurance. Homes are already wired to enable the fitting of an electric car charging point free of charge within the first two years of moving in if residents make the switch to electric.

Other sustainable travel options include the launch of the Elmsbrook Brompton Bike Loan Scheme, providing free flexible bike hire, enabling residents to borrow one of four folding bikes a week at a time.

On the back of these successful launch initiatives at Elmsbrook, A2Dominion is looking forward to exploring innovative new technologies to enable true zero-carbon living and take the next steps with phase two launching this year.

14 March 2017

⇨ The above information is reprinted with kind permission from 24housing. Please visit www.24housing.co.uk for further information.

What is the future for sustainable homes in the UK?

By Sharon Russell-Verma

We repeatedly hear in the media that there is a housing shortage in the UK. With a growing population particularly in urban areas, we need to be smart about addressing this need. A couple of weeks ago I wrote about the recent scrapping of the zero-carbon homes policy but there is another policy, the code for sustainable homes (CSH) that has also been scrapped. Like the zero-carbon homes policy it was developed to help achieve more sustainable homes. So, where does that leave the ability to provide an adequate supply of sustainable homes for our needs today and our children's needs in the future?

What makes a house a sustainable home?

Firstly, let's be clear about what we mean by a sustainable home. The idea of sustainable development was coined back in 1987 and is defined as development that meets the needs of the present without compromising the needs of future generations. So a sustainable home should work within this definition and should:

⇨ be designed to reduce environmental impact during and after construction

⇨ use energy, water, land and other resources efficiently

⇨ protect the occupant's health and,

⇨ reduce pollution, waste and greenhouse gases.

The code for sustainable homes

In 2006 when the code for sustainable homes was launched the aim was to set standards to be used across the house-building industry. The CSH had nine categories of sustainable design and construction, developed to reflect the requirements of sustainable homes and lifestyles:

⇨ Energy and CO inf. Emissions

⇨ Water

⇨ Materials

⇨ Surface Water Run-off

⇨ Waste

⇨ Pollution

⇨ Health and Well-being

⇨ Management

⇨ Ecology.

The categories above, together with a star-rating system, were used communicate the overall sustainability performance. Home designs could achieve level 1 to 6, with 6 being the highest level. To achieve a 6 the home needed to be zero carbon (i.e. zero net emissions of CO_2 from all energy use in the home). The code itself was voluntary and councils around the UK had the freedom to adopt their own sustainability levels for new residential development, with code level 3, 4, 5 or 6 as potential planning conditions. According to the Government, the code was scrapped in order to reduce the burden of regulations on house builders.

Yet, the CSH had its benefits; as mentioned, it gave local authorities the ability to demand homes of higher quality in their areas. Furthermore, the CSH led the way towards more sustainable housing construction; it stimulated a reduction in the price of residential micro-generation technologies

such as solar PV. It also helped to develop and improve the skills and knowledge in the housing construction sector. In fact, many house builders have adopted some or all of the of sustainable design and construction categories that contribute to a home's level of sustainability. Today, there are homes across the UK which are being built to the code 6 level. Let's take a look at one example Bicester's Eco-town project.

Case study – Eco-town, Bicester

The Eco-town near Bicester is built on a 51-acre site with 40% of the land in the development devoted to green space. This green area encourages the people living there to enjoy an outdoor lifestyle, to nurture a love of wildlife and increase biodiversity. The green area also provides safe playing areas area for children. There are local cycle routes and pedestrian routes to encourage people to have a healthier lifestyle. Community allotments allow space for residents to grow their own food and engage socially as well as providing a space for communal events. The Eco-town has charging points for electric vehicles and an electric car club. In addition there is a bus service within 400 metres of every home with live timetable updates in each house via computer screen. The project has been designed to ensure that zero waste goes to landfill during its development to align it with sustainability targets.

The environmental technology within the houses is inspiring too, including rainwater harvesting, water recycling, solar PV panels and triple glazing. Each house also comes complete with a computer system that displays the energy usage of the house in real time as well as the local transport information. Other sustainable features included in the Eco-town project are meadow turf roofs to encourage biodiversity, an energy centre supplying combined heat and power to all homes, with any extra power exported to the national grid. All in all this is a great example of a housing project that demonstrates the key principles of sustainability by incorporating the economic,

the social and the environmental needs of the people that live there with as little impact on the environment as possible and maybe even enhancing it in some ways.

What's next for sustainable homes, standards?

So with no standards to adhere to, where does the housing industry go from here? Well, the good news is that some elements of the code (including energy requirements) will now be incorporated into the building regulations. They will be re-named "the new national technical standards" and set at a minimum equivalent of a CSH level 4.

In the meantime BRE (Building Research Establishment) has said it will continue to certify schemes under the CSH. At the same time they are developing a new national home quality mark (HQM) which will be launched in October 2015. The quality mark is designed to give house buyers independent and clear information on a new home's quality. It should give house buyers clear indications of the expected costs to run the house, how the home will benefit their health and well-being, and the environmental footprint of living in the home.

This is a good start but it does not reflect the more stringent requirements of the old code. While the old code may have been harder to meet, many house builders were and are rising to the challenge. This in the long run will benefit them as companies, their customers and the environment. If sustainable homes are to improve above and beyond what they have already achieved it is also up to us, the house buyer, to demand more, for today's generation and future generations.

11 August 2015

⇨ The above information is reprinted with kind permission from YouGen. Please visit www.yougen. co.uk for further information.

The village revival

An extract from the report by Strutt & Parker.

The world might be focused on urbanisation, but a new, overlooked trend is set to shape the UK's housing market

A cursory glance at existing research would suggest cities have the upper hand over villages. By 2050, the UN predicts that 66% of the world's population will be urban, with the UK inevitably being part of the trent. By mid-century, there will be approximately 65 million people living in Britain's cities, compared to just eight million in rural areas.

Urbanisation has generally been viewed as a positive economic and social driver that leads to longer life expectancies, a reduction in poverty, increased literacy and higher education levels, as well as enhanced cultural opportunities.

But as the urban trend has gathered pace, a number of negative traits have begun to appear. When urbanisation is too rapid, or when it is undertaken without proper planning, cities can become more unequal than rural areas, resulting in a rise in substandard living conditions, urban sprawl and increased pollution. Urbanisation can also lead to unsustainable production and consumption patterns.

Add in concerns about the affordability of housing and limited development, and perhaps it is not so surprising that over the past three years of Housing Futures research we have seen the emergence of a new creeping trend – the desire to move back to rural. In our latest research, 21% of respondents who are moving want to live in a village, making it easily the most popular location. The shift away from cities is being driven by people looking for neighbourhood safety (86%) and space between neighbours (58%), as well as for a strong community feel (48%).

According to Defra, in 2013/14, the UK saw net internal migration of 60,000 people to predominantly rural areas in England. It is a trend that has been positive every year since 2001. But this reverse migration is not to a traditional rural environment. The influence that technology is having on shopping, communications and, most importantly, working habits is helping to transform villages and the type of people who want to live in them.

Technology is also helping to change the rural economy, which plays a key role in creating jobs and prosperity. England's rural economy now accounts for £210 billion of economic output and hosts over 25% of all registered businesses.

Once the preserve of agricultural enterprises, new companies are thriving in rural locations, including hi-tech manufacturing, food processing, the service sector, retail and power supply (in the form of renewables). What's more, the expansion of broadband and mobile communications has seen a greater uptake of working from home in rural locations compared to urban areas.

It seems the same factors that once drove urbanisation – improving economic and social conditions – are now inspiring the village revival.

Village tribes

The Downtons

The most prestigious house in the village would once have been owned by the local squire. Many of these properties have now been acquired by buyers using property equity to purchase a rural idyll. Of those Strutt & Parker clients who are buying outside of London in the £2 million-plus bracket, 98% say they would want the property to be a house or an estate/farm estate. Today, not everyone wants to buy the rural lifestyle – some would prefer to rent it. *Spear's Wealth Management* has identified a trend for wealthy, shorter-term renters looking for services normally found in private members' clubs, for example properties that feature 'butler buzzers' in every room.

Elderflowers

Born after the Second World War, the Elderflowers have benefited from sustained economic growth, as well as increasing levels of housing equity. They are the largest demographic in the UK – and they are growing. By 2033, 60% of household growth will be headed by those aged 65 or over. Elderflowers have either lived in the village all their lives or are empty nesters looking to move into a village house that suits their changing needs. Skilled and experienced, they are able to take advantage of the flexible work styles suitable to the modern village. As a healthy and active generation, the Elderflowers are in a position to enjoy a positive move into and through retirement.

Rusticarians

These diverse countryside dwellers embrace new approaches to work and lifestyle. For example, rural areas have the highest rate of homeworkers – 33% compared to 12% in urban areas. These homeworkers tend to be employed in higher-skilled roles and are part of a wider group of rural entrepreneurs. Research from Defra, published in January 2015, points out that the number of businesses registered per head of population is higher in predominantly rural areas than predominantly urban surroundings. Technology is key to this group, with 49% of those intending to move to a village citing broadband as the main motivation for moving, up from 41% in 2014.

Rubies

Attracting new residents, particularly adults with children, is vital for a village. That's why Rubies – or Rural Newbies – are an important village tribe. This group of predominantly younger families supports the local school, uses community facilities for classes and leisure activities, and sustains local shops. However, the affordability of housing is a challenge. In England, 59% of those aged 25–34 owned their home in 2003/4, but ten years later it was just 36%. Over the same period, renting for this age group grew from 21% to 48%. The good news is that Help to Buy is having a positive impact, with 81% of mortgages completed supporting first-time buyers.

The Onesies

Single-person households are growing ten times faster than the general population. It is estimated that by 2033, sole occupiers will make up 41% of all households. This trend is driven by several factors, including rising life expectancy and divorce, and particularly reflects the requirements of older women. About 3.8 million older people are single-dwellers and 70% of these are women. The challenge is to provide suitable housing options for Onesies. These range from individuals who need to downsize as they occupy a home that is too large for their requirements to people seeking more spacious options than those offered by a one-bedroom flat.

2016

⇨ The above information is reprinted with kind permission from Strutt & Parker. Please visit www.struttandparker.com/housingfutures for further information.

14 garden villages to be built in England totalling 48,000 homes

Sites for new villages include green belt-land and spread from Cornwall to Cumbria, but local opposition is strong in some areas.

By Jessica Elgot

Some 14 garden villages are to be built across England on sites including a former airfield and green-belt land, ministers have said.

The villages, totalling 48,000 homes, will not be extensions of existing small towns or villages, but "distinct new places with their own community facilities", the Government said.

Sites from Cornwall to Cumbria have been identified in the first round of approved locations, making them eligible for a share of a £6 million government technical and financial support fund. After completion, the villages may vary in size from 1,500 homes up to 10,000.

Missed opportunities of garden villages plan

The housing minister, Gavin Barwell, said the development of the villages would be locally led by communities rather than central government. "New communities not only deliver homes, they also bring new jobs and facilities and a big boost to local economies," he said.

The 600-acre former Deenethorpe airfield near Corby, Northamptonshire, is one of the sites that has been approved for a village. The plans include a village green, shops and community hall, as well as more than 1,000 homes.

Dunton Hills, a garden village set to be built near Brentwood, Essex, will have at least 2,500 homes, as well as new Gypsy and Traveller pitches.

West Carclaze in Cornwall is set to be an ecovillage with 1,500 new energy-efficient homes, space for self-build and custom-built housing, and a new primary school for more than 400 pupils.

Developers say it will have a solar farm and 350 hectares of green space in a new china clay heritage park incorporating the Sky Tip, a local landmark. Bike trails and pubs are also planned.

However, local councillors have raised concerns about the small percentage of affordable housing and change in character of the historical mining area.

Councillor Dick Cole, leader of the Cornish devolution party Mebyon Kernow, who said he had objected to proposals for an ecotown for a decade, said the garden village announcement was no more than window dressing for a controversial project.

"The Government talks about it being a locally led development, but the reality is that this is only happening because it was a government top-down initiative," he told *The Guardian*.

"They say it is a brownfield site, but many of the houses are on fields. It has been one of those projects that seems to have a momentum of its own, despite what local people say."

North Cheshire garden village, which will sit on the eastern edge of Handforth, has development plans that include 2,000 homes, a nursery and a care home, as well as architect-designed 'one-off' homes.

However, locals are worried that a new village of several thousand homes may put pressure on infrastructure such as the congested A34.

Other planned villages include Long Marston in Warwickshire, Spitalgate Heath in Lincolnshire, Bailrigg in Lancaster and the Infinity Garden Village in Derbyshire.

The final six are Oxfordshire Cotswold, Culm in Devon, Welborne in Hampshire, Halsnead in Merseyside, Longcross in Surrey and St Cuthberts near Carlisle.

The garden village initiative was announced by the then chancellor George Osborne last year. Conditions for building villages or market towns stated that the developments must be "a new discrete settlement and not an extension of an existing town or village".

Shaun Spiers, the chief executive of the Campaign to Protect Rural England (CPRE), said it would carefully examine the proposals to see whether they were locally led and respected the green belt.

"Done well with genuine local consent, garden villages and towns can help tackle the housing crisis," he said. "They can certainly be preferable to what is currently happening in too many parts of the country: poor quality developments plonked on the countryside, in the teeth of local opposition and in defiance of good planning principles."

But areas that absorbed the new garden villages should have guarantees that they would be "protected from speculative planning applications for a long time to come", he added.

The Department for Communities and Local Government said there had been high levels of interest in building more

villages in the coming years and it would make an additional £1 million available this year to further development other proposals.

Three new garden towns have also been announced near Aylesbury in Buckinghamshire, Taunton in Somerset and Harlow and Gilston in Hertfordshire, with £1.4 million of funding to support the delivery of about 50,000 homes.

Local CPRE members strongly object to the Hertfordshire plans, under which

the village of Gilston and neighbouring hamlet of Eastwick would disappear.

Kevin FitzGerald, the honorary director of CPRE Hertfordshire, said: "These plans herald the death knell of the rural character of whole swaths of Hertfordshire. Beautiful villages, supposedly protected by green belt [designation], look set to be swallowed up by the urban sprawl of neighbouring towns.

"Housing targets are putting immense pressure on our area and marginalising

the basic purposes of the green belt, which the Government has pledged to protect."

2 January 2017

⇨ The above information is reprinted with kind permission from *The Guardian*. Please visit www.theguardian.com for further information.

Flatpack homes: the future of social housing?

By Jenna Kamal

"**H**ousing today is perhaps the most important form of social exclusion – and arguably the defining issue of our time."

– Jack Self, Co-curator, the British Pavilion, Venice Biennale 2016

The housing crisis was one of the central topics in Phillip Hammond's Autumn Statement however, critics have argued that the outlined changes to combat the housing crisis were not enough. Dawn Foster, for example, wrote, "Hammond's announcement of £4 billion to fund new affordable homes was a headline-grabbing number. As always, though, it's worth reading the small print: the £1.4 billion tranche earmarked for local authorities to provide new affordable homes specifies the homes built can be shared-ownership schemes, or affordable rent (that is, don't forget 80% of the local market rent), but not social rent, which in many areas is the only truly affordable housing tenure."

The Guardian argues that the reality of affordable housing paints a "worrying picture". "The Government's figures show that affordable housing delivery was 52% lower in 2015–2016 compared with the previous year."

However, some leading architects have taken social housing back to the drawing board, and the results have been global. London, Bristol, Chile and Australia have adopted some aspect of flatpack houses. Marketed as a stepping stone out of homelessness,

"first-home owners or low-income households, and people interested in sustainable houses".

The pop-up village: Lewisham, 2016

⇨ With a staggering 9,135 households on its waiting list for homes, the borough came up with the solution of a £4.3 million scheme "to provide 24 homes and 880 sq metres of business space that can be picked up and moved at a later date, allowing the council to make use of vacant brownfield land while longer-term projects are finalised".

⇨ The units, which are built in a factory and transported to the site, have a lifespan of 60 years.

⇨ "The flats have cost £1,200 per sq metres to make and fit out with kitchens, white goods and bathrooms, working out at £90,000 for each home. Harbour said building them in a factory rather than onsite allowed costs to be kept down. The lightweight timber construction has also meant savings, as the foundations only need to be half as deep as for equivalent brick-built blocks. They have a lifespan of 60 years and can be moved several times in that period and configured however the council needs them to be."

⇨ The development, which the council has branded as "the UK's first pop-up village" were a

solution to "rapidly rising property prices and rents, combined with the loss of social housing through right to buy". The result of these issues "have put councils under growing pressure to find new ways to help people off their housing lists".

Tackling homelessness: Bristol, 2016

⇨ Replicating Lewisham's pop-up village, Bristol might start witnessing similar flatpack houses, aiming to tackle "the city's problem with homelessness".

⇨ Bristol councillor Paul Smith said the pop-up accommodation is a "creative" way of helping the city's homeless.

⇨ Mr Smith said "the pop-up accommodation would be a 'temporary solution, not a long-term solution' to homelessness".

The Y-Cube: Wimbledon, 2014:

⇨ In 2014, Richard Rogers collaborated with the YMCA to create £30,000 flatpack homes for homeless people.

⇨ According to its makers, the dwelling, which was airlifted onto a side street in Wimbledon, "could be the answer to the housing crisis… providing a first step for those in desperate need for accommodation".

⇨ Andy Redfearn of the YMCA explained, "The real issue is

what happens when people leave our hostels." "The only option is often poor-quality shared accommodation managed by private landlords, who require large deposits and rent in advance."

⇨ The timber used is glue-laminated and cut with precision, making the units packed with insulations.

⇨ The units can be stacked on top of one another to form an eight-storey-high block.

⇨ "The precision construction means a degree of air-tightness that brings the units to level 6 of the code for sustainable homes: a three-week test showed each home can be lit and heated to 20°C all day and all night for £7 per week. The system also allows for units to be joined, windows cut into corners and partition walls freely arranged within, bringing more flexibility than the usual container-home – and built with a lifespan of 60 years."

The ZEDpod: London, 2016

⇨ The award-winning architecture practice, Zed Factory, have created the ZEDpod: "Low-cost prefabricated pod homes."

⇨ Built on stilts above car parks, the proposal is to create low-cost, environmentally friendly housing.

⇨ "If a site later became earmarked for development, [it] could simply be transported to another location."

⇨ The development would be cheap to run, equipped with solar panels, water-recycling systems and even "on-site charging points for electric vehicles".

⇨ "At a cost of £60,000 each to build, they are intended as affordable starter and rental homes, their size dictated by that of two car parking bays below."

⇨ "They could, however, still be rented out for an estimated £650 to £750 per month."

Modulhus: for the first time Buyer, 2016

⇨ These "pre-built, customisable homes are being touted as a way

to help get first-time buyers onto the property ladder".

⇨ "A far cry from the low-quality post-Second World War prefab houses, new technology means that factory-built houses can be at the cutting-edge of architecture – functional, sustainable and generally more affordable than traditional brick."

⇨ "TV property experts Kevin McCloud, Charlie Luxton and George Clarke awarded it the winner of the Starter Home on a Shoestring competition, run by the National Custom & Self Build Association."

⇨ The design is pre-built in a factory and then transported to the desired site. The assembly can take just a few days.

⇨ "There is no need for internal structural support so just about any interior layout can be accommodated."

⇨ "With possible savings of up to 30 per cent on buying an existing property, including buying the land, this could bring the average cost of first-time buyer homes down to £300,000 from £430,000 in London, and £175,000 from £250,000 nationwide."

Modular Architectural Adaptable Panel: Australia, 2016

⇨ Designed and manufactured by Daniel Reitsma and Edward Duc, this flatpack house was built like Lego, "if you use the same-sized pieces you can build what you want".

⇨ "Buyers can add to the layout later by adding rooms when they can afford to."

⇨ Their construction of the "three-bedroom, two-bathroom prototype home initially took eight weeks, with a team of five".

⇨ Mr Duc, the architect involved in the project explains, "In traditional construction up to 30 per cent of the materials and labour is wasted – houses use more energy than any other type of building in the world."

⇨ "The only way we will be able to house people satisfactorily is to produce houses in factories."

Chile: Half a House, 2010

⇨ "With a magnitude of 8.8, the quake that hit Constitución was the second biggest that the world had seen in half a century. The quake and the tsunami it produced completely crushed the town. By the time it was over, more than 500 people were dead, and about 80% of the Constitución's buildings were ruined."

⇨ As part of the relief effort, architect Alejandro Aravena reshaped the concept of social housing by providing victims half a house.

⇨ "They are cheaper to build, and easier to construct, than traditional social housing. But crucially, they also allow the homeowners themselves to invest in the property to bring it up to a middle-class standard: the exact same process that happens without guidance (and indeed often against the law) in informal settlements around the world."

⇨ "In the context of Chile, Aravena's ideas empowered a group of people whose lives were devastated by a natural disaster – the 2010 tsunami. In the British context, of course, Jack Self points out that handing ownership of social housing to the people who live there was the reasoning behind the right-to-buy policy – which has been an unmitigated disaster for anyone who needs social housing but wasn't lucky enough to ride the first wave of selloffs." (11)

6 December 2016

⇨ The above information is reprinted with kind permission from Property Moose. Please visit www.propertymoose.co.uk for further information.

© *Property Moose 2017*

London microflats could be the answer to people wanting to live in Zone One

By Sarah Ann Harris

Some Londoners might at last be able to afford to live in Zone One thanks to a new range of "micro-flats" proposed by a regeneration specialist.

A "compact living" scheme, offering residents pint-sized apartments with a floor size of either 19 or 24 square metres, is coming to the capital.

Town Flats, marketed as ideal for young professionals, will cost between £700-£1,200 per month, with at least 50% falling within the London Living Rent.

London Living Rent is a scheme to help people currently renting, who earn between £30,000 and £60,000, to build up their savings in order to buy a home.

Town Flats will be rental only, meaning they cannot be bought and sold, and will be built in partnership with local authorities making best use of currently redundant public sector land, which will remain in public ownership.

In a report by Development Economics, commissioned by U+I, it was found that Town flats would provide 4,770 more homes, based on an assumption of locating five town flat development sites in each of the nine inner London boroughs.

U+I Deputy Chief Executive, Richard Upton, said: "For too long and for too many people London has been hollowing itself out - diluting the rich blend which has made it the global capital. The centre is now only affordable to either the very wealthy, only occasionally present, or those living in what social housing remains.

"For a new generation of workers in the middle, often working centrally, living in the middle of London has long been a dream.

"People increasingly want to live, work and play in the same place and we want to develop something that not only re-fills hollow London, but also brings communities back to life and delivers real social and economic benefits.

"Ideally we would like to develop these sites in association with public sector bodies who have unused land. This could bring additional social benefit to the public sector by generating much needed revenue from the rental income, while retaining ownership of their assets."

Small living quarters have also previously prompted the likes of the Royal Institute of British Architects and Shelter to express their concern about so-called "rabbit hutch" accommodation.

U+I has built test flats in its headquarters, furnished by John Lewis, who is now creating a whole range for people living in small spaces.

The next step will be for U+I to find a landowner to partner with for the project.

13 September 2017

⇨ The above information is reprinted with kind permission from The Huffington Post UK. Please visit www.huffingtonpost.co.uk for further information.

Key facts

⇨ Some 76% of people who do not own their own home expect to do so in the next five years (page 1)

⇨ Almost two thirds of people (64%) are very happy with their homes, awarding them a 4 or 5 star rating. (page 2)

⇨ Home owners are noticeably happier (74%) than non-owners (55%). (page 2)

⇨ Half (50%) of millennials work from home and almost a third (29%) would like to, whereas only a third (33%) of baby boomers work from home and only 16% would like to. (page 2)

⇨ In the early twentieth century, 76% of all households lived in privately rented accommodation. (page 3)

⇨ For the least wealthy, property accounted for 34% of total wealth in 2012-14, whereas for the wealthiest it accounted for 31%. (page 3)

⇨ In Malaysia, this figure rises to more than three-quarters (77%) of millennials. This is lowest in the UAE at 45%. (page 1)

⇨ It should come as no surprise therefore that more than half (53%) of recent home owners found the total cost of buying a home was more than they had budgeted. (page 2)

⇨ Amongst unemployed people, the largest proportion (27%) are living in housing association provided accommodation. There are also just over 13% of unemployed people buying a house with a mortgage. (page 3)

⇨ Between 1983 and 2016, first-time buyer house prices have been on average, 3.5 times earnings. (page 4)

⇨ Between 1999 and 2014 the number living with their parents rose by one million – faster than the rate of population growth for that age group. (page 4)

⇨ The under-35s bear the largest mortgage debt – averaging £91,000 per person in England. (page 4)

⇨ The average UK house price was £214,000 in June 2016 (page 5)

⇨ The percentage of 25- to 29-year-olds owning their home decreased from 55% in 1996 to 29% in 2015 (page 5)

⇨ For decades, successive governments have failed to build the homes we need. By 2008, the number of new homes being started had fallen to its lowest peacetime level since 1924 – and house building has barely recovered since then. (page 6)

⇨ The latest English Housing Survey, produced by the Department for Communities and Local Government (DCLG), found that of the estimated 22.8 million households in England, 14.3 million– or 62.9% – were owner-occupiers in 2015–16. (page 8)

⇨ Government data reveals that the private rented sector has doubled in size since 2004, with almost half of all people in England aged 25 to 34 paying a private landlord for their accommodation. (page 8)

⇨ While the proportion of people with a mortgage falls dramatically with age, there is still a small minority of people with a mortgage between the ages of 65-75 (around 5%). (page 3)

⇨ A total of 14,420 households were accepted by local authorities as homeless between October and December 2016, up by more than half since 2009 – with 78% of the increase since 2011 being the result of people losing their previous private tenancy (page 14)

⇨ Across the UK the charity has calculated that, if the housing benefit freeze remains in place as planned until 2020, more than a million households, including 375,000 with at least one person in work, could be forced out of their homes. It estimates that 211,000 households in which no one works because of disability could be forced to go. (page 14)

⇨ Government statistics reveal that since the Tories came to power in 2010, homelessness and the number of people living in temporary accommodation has risen dramatically. (page 16)

⇨ In June 2010, the number of families with children living in B&Bs for more than six weeks was 160. (page 16)

⇨ Within the M25 that circles greater London there are 110,000 hectares of green-belt land. If we built on just one quarter of this land, we could provide more than one million new homes. (page 17)

⇨ But today, the UK is experiencing a housing crisis. The nation requires 220,000 new homes each year to keep up with demand – not to mention making up for the undersupply from previous years. In the year to September 2016, only 141,000 were built. This deficit has sparked renewed debate over the value of the green belt. (page 23)

⇨ Just over 65 million people reside in the UK. England is the most populous nation with 54 million people, most of whom live in urban neighbourhoods. (page 29)

Bedroom Tax

A change in housing benefit to pay less money to those in a council or housing association property that is considered to have one or more spare rooms.

Eco-friendly

A change in housing benefit to pay less money to those in a council or housing association property that is considered to have one or more spare rooms.

Greenbelt land

A policy to prevent urban sprawls into rural areas - designates land which must remain largely undeveloped.

Help-to-buy

A scheme offered by the government that gives prospective home-buyers the opportunity to take out an interest-free loan or where the government acts as a guarantor for some of the borrower's debt.

Homelessness

The law defines somebody as being homeless if they do not have a legal right to occupy any accommodation or if their accommodation is unsuitable to live in. This can cover a wide range of circumstances, including, but not restricted to, the following: having no accommodation at all; having accommodation that is not reasonable to live in, even in the short-term (e.g. because of violence or health reasons); having a legal right to accommodation that for some reason you cannot access (e.g. if you have been illegally evicted); living in accommodation you have no legal right to occupy (e.g. living in a squat or temporarily staying with friends).

Hidden Homelessness

In addition to those people recognised as statutory homeless there are also a large number of homeless single adults, or couples without dependent children, who meet the legal definition of homelessness but not the criteria for priority need. In many cases they will not even apply for official recognition, knowing they do not meet the criteria. Statistics provided by the Government will therefore not include all people in the country who actually meet the definition of homelessness. As a result, this group is often referred to as the hidden homeless.

Housing Benefit

Money provided by the government to help meet housing costs for rented accommodation for those that would be unable to do so alone.

Housing Deposit

An amount of money paid to secure a property.

Mortgage

A loan taken out to pay for a property which is paid back with interest.

Owner/Occupier

An occupant that owns the home they live in.

Social Housing

Accommodation which is owned by the government or local authority and then rented to tenants with the aim of providing affordable housing.

Sustainable

Something that is capable of being maintained at a particular rate or level.

Assignments

Brainstorming

⇨ As a class discuss what you know about housing in the UK.

- What is a mortgage?

- What does it mean to rent a property?

- What is social housing?

- What is homelessness?

Research

⇨ Research private renting in the UK. How much do people pay in rent on average in different parts of the country. Produce a graph to show your findings.

⇨ Talk to your friends and their families and your relatives to find out how many people own their properties. Make a note of the different age groups who are home owners, how long they have taken out a mortgage for, and how much it costs each month. Write some notes on your findings and share with the rest of the class.

⇨ Do you live in a village or town? Ask your classmates where they live. What percentage live in a village? What percentage live in a town? Produce an infogram showing your findings.

⇨ Research how much people need to buy their first home. What percentage is needed for the deposit? How much are solicitors fees on average? What different types of home survey can people have done and what is the difference in cost between them? Produce a graph to show your findings.

⇨ Choose a country in Europe and look at their housing situation. Do more people rent than own? Is there a housing shortage? Compare your findings with the rest of the class.

⇨ Research the average purchase price of a 3-bedroom semi-detached house in different parts of the country. Produce a graph to show your findings.

Design

⇨ In small groups design a property. It is entirely up to each group whether they design a house, bunglaow or flat. Consider if it is going to be 'eco-friendly'. Will the building have all the latest technology incorporated into it? Share your designs with the rest of the class.

⇨ Design a poster highlighting the problem of homelessness. Your aim is to make people aware of this problem and show some of the reasons why people become homeless.

⇨ Look at the illustration on page 14 and design your own illustration to replace it.

⇨ You are a develper who is building 200 eco-friendly homes. In groups design a leaflet giving potential buyers information about the homes.

Oral

⇨ Divide the class in half. Debate renting versus ownership of property. One group should argue for renting and the other for ownership.

⇨ Read the article 'Private tenants are putting up with dangerously cold homes, scared of eviction if they complain'. Discuss this in small groups. What do you think you would do if this happened to you? Do you think you might be confident enough to complain?

⇨ As a class discuss the housing crisis in the UK. What does the term 'housing crisis' mean? What do you think can be done to overcome this crisis?

⇨ In small groups discuss the benefits of living in a town rather than a village.

Reading/Writing

⇨ Imagine you are a single mother/father and have been forced to live in a B&B with your 2 children. Write a blog which should explore your feelings about the situation.

⇨ Do you agree with houses being built on green spaces? Write a two-page article giving your views on this. Why do you feel the way you do about this issue?

⇨ An application has been made to build a development of 150 new homes in your village. Write a letter to your MP giving the reasons you are against this development. In your letter you should consider the impact on local schools, doctor's surgeries etc.

⇨ Write a one-paragraph definition of the term 'garden village'.

⇨ What does the term 'shortage of affordable homes' mean? Write a one-page article explaining this term.

⇨ Read the article on page 10 about private renting. Imagine you are a landlord. Write a letter to a tenant advising them of their rights and responsibilities as a tenant.

⇨ Imagine you are a tenant and your landlord is not maintaining the property you live in properly. Write him/her a letter telling them you are not happy with the way things are being handled. List the problems you have with the property and suggest a meeting to discuss the issues.

Acknowledgements

The publisher is grateful for permission to reproduce the material in this book. While every care has been taken to trace and acknowledge copyright, the publisher tenders its apology for any accidental infringement or where copyright has proved untraceable. The publisher would be pleased to come to a suitable arrangement in any such case with the rightful owner.

Images

All images courtesy of iStock except pages 19, 32, 33, 36 and 39: Pixabay, page 35 (top) © Brandon Morgan and page 35 (bottom) © Corina Ardeleaunu.

Icons

Icons on page 1 were made by Freepik from www.flaticon.com.

Illustrations

Don Hatcher: pages 2 & 30. Simon Kneebone: pages 11 & 25. Angelo Madrid: pages 5 & 14.

Additional acknowledgements

Editorial on behalf of Independence Educational Publishers by Cara Acred.

With thanks to the Independence team: Shelley Baldry, Tina Brand, Sandra Dennis, Jackie Staines and Jan Sunderland.

Cara Acred

Cambridge, September 2017

About *ISSUES*

ISSUES is a unique series of cross-curricular resource books for 14- to 18-year-olds. The series explores contemporary social issues, stimulating debate among readers of all levels. Each book presents a range of facts and opinions, providing the reader with an unbiased overview of the topic.

Titles contain articles and statistics from all key players involved in the topic covered, and include a range of diverse opinions. Elements include:

- Key facts
- Magazine features
- Charity group literature
- Cartoons and illustrations
- Journal and book extracts
- Extracts from government reports
- Statistics, including tables and graphs
- Newspaper reports and feature articles
- Accessible, easy to photocopy, full colour layouts
- Glossaries, timelines and diagrams

Independence Educational Publishers

Orders can be placed directly with the publisher:

Independence, The Studio,
High Green, Great Shelford,
Cambridge, CB22 5EG, England

Fax: 01223 550806
Phone: 01223 550801
www.independence.co.uk

Email:
issues@independence.co.uk

RRP: £7.95

ISBN 978-1-86168-775-3

Student Life

Editor: Tina Brand

Volume 333

ISSUES